westermann

Qualifikationsphase
Sekundarstufe II

Pathway
Advanced
Special

We the People?
America – A Nation Fighting Itself

Herausgegeben von:
Iris Edelbrock

Erarbeitet von:
Iris Edelbrock

Sprachlich betreut von:
John Poziemski
Ellen King

How to work with the book

Symbols & skills

Group work, work in a team, work with a partner
→ communication skills

Communication training, e. g. discussion, debate, role play, hot seat, etc.
→ communication skills

Mediation between English and German
→ mediation skills

Creative writing task
→ writing skills

Presentation of projects, results of group work or research
→ speaking skills

Tasks for advanced students

@ **Internet research**
→ intercultural competences

Level of difficulty

●○○ basic

●●○ intermediate

●●● advanced

westermann GRUPPE

Druck A[1] / Jahr 2020
Alle Drucke der Serie A sind im Unterricht parallel verwendbar.

Redaktion: Marion Kramer
Umschlaggestaltung: Westermann, Fotos: Rob Casey/Alamy Stock Foto (vorn);
Zoonar GmbH/Alamy Stock Foto (hinten)
Druck und Bindung: Westermann Druck GmbH, Braunschweig

ISBN 978-3-14-**040228**-6

Contents

We the People? ... Divisions and Disparities

Protesters marching in a solidarity rally reenact the scene in which George Floyd was arrested by police in Minneapolis New York City, 2 June 2020

Tips on vocab

Photo: to re-enact a scene ■ to gather around sb. ■ to kneel on sb.'s neck ■ to lie facedown ■ to have one's hands tied together behind one's back ■ to raise one's fist ■ to have a bleak facial expression ■ to suffocate (sb.)

Cartoon: to lie facedown under a police car ■ Lady Justice blindfolded ■ to (usually) hold up scales ■ to symbolize morality and justice ■ to lie scattered on the street ■ to kneel on sb.'s neck ■ to have one's hands in one's pockets ■ to appear indifferent and unemotional

START-UP ACTIVITIES

1. Describe the photo and explain
   a) what exactly the protesters are 're-enact-ing' and
   b) the message the scene conveys.

2. Compare the message of the photo to the cartoon:
   a) How does the cartoonist present the brutal behaviour of the police?
   b) Which violations of civil and human rights does the cartoon denounce (*anprangern*)?

James Baldwin

Cambridge University Debate – 1965

[...] Let me put it this way: that from a very literal[1] point of view, the harbors and the ports and the railroads of the country; the economy, especially of the Southern States, could not conceivably[2] be what it has become if they had not had, and do not still have, indeed, and for so long – so many generations – cheap labor. [...]

It is a terrible thing for an entire people to surrender[3] to the notion[4] that one-ninth of its population is beneath them. And until that moment, until the moment comes when we the Americans, we the American people, are able to accept the fact that I have to accept, for example, that my ancestors are both white and black, that on that continent we are trying to forge[5] a new identity for which we need each other, and that I am not a ward[6] of America, I am not an object of missionary[7] charity, I am one of the people who built the country. Until this moment, there is scarcely[8] any hope for the American dream, because the people who are denied participation in it, by their very presence, will wreck it. And if that happens, it is a very grave[9] moment for the West. Thank you.

James Baldwin

The Negro and the American Promise – 1963

[...] I can't be a pessimist, because I'm alive. To be a pessimist means that you have agreed that human life is an academic matter. So I'm forced to be an optimist. I'm forced to believe that we can survive whatever we must survive. But the Negro in this country ... the future of the Negro in this country is precisely as bright or as dark as the future of the country. It is entirely up to the American people and our representatives – it is entirely up to the American people whether or not they are going to face and deal with and embrace this stranger whom they maligned[10] so long. What white people have to do is try and find out in their own hearts why it was necessary to have a nigger in the first place, because I'm not a nigger, I'm a man[11]. But if you think I'm a nigger, it means you need it. The question you've got to ask yourself, the white population of this country has got to ask itself, North and South because it's one country and for a Negro there is no difference between the North and the South – it's just a difference in the way they castrate[12] you, but the fact of the castration is the American fact ... If I'm not the nigger here and you invented him, you, the white people invented him, then you've got to find out why. And the future of the country depends on that, whether or not it is able to ask that question.

from *I Am Not Your Negro* by James Baldwin and Raoul Peck. Based on the film *I Am Not Your Negro* © 2016 by Velvet Film, Inc. and Velvet Film SAS. Penguin, New York 2017, pp. 77, 108 f.

3. As one of the most prominent African American writers and civil rights activists of his time, James Baldwin (1924 – 1987) critically examined the treatment of African Americans throughout U. S. history.
Read the two excerpts from Baldwin's statements and
a) point out the importance for the 'West' to "forge a new identity" and to enable black people to participate in the American Dream.
b) explain why the American people and politicians should "face and deal with and embrace this stranger".

4. Discuss Baldwin's statement that the white people "invented" the "nigger" and that it was necessary for them to "have a nigger".

[1] **literal** here: matter-of-fact; *sachlich, objektiv* – [2] **conceivably** possibly – [3] **to surrender** to stop fighting and admit defeat – [4] **notion** a belief or idea – [5] **to forge** to produce or make sth., esp. with some difficulty – [6] **ward** *Schutzbefohlener, Mündel* – [7] **missionary** *missionarisch* – [8] **scarcely** almost not – [9] **grave** seriously bad – [10] **to malign sb./sth.** to say false and unpleasant things about sb./sth. – [11] **man** here: human being – [12] **to castrate sb.** *kastrieren*; here: to disenfranchise sb. (*jdn. entrechten*)

Guido Mingels et al.

A Perfect Storm: Democracy on the Defensive in Trump's America

AWARENESS

Team up with a partner and describe the cartoon below.

- Which disasters and crises in U. S. history does the little girl refer to?
- Explain the implication that Americans have been/are experiencing "all [of this] at once".

Tips on vocab

grandfather ■ to sit in an armchair ■ to study a history book ■ to have a concerned facial expression ■ to shed a tear ■ granddaughter with ponytail ■ bulging eyes ■ to be scared ■ when it rains, it pours (*prov.*) ■ a series of disasters

Coronavirus, economic collapse and now mass demonstrations for racial equality: The United States is facing a trio of deep crises. Instead of offering leadership, President Donald Trump is exacerbating[1] divisions and showing authoritarian tendencies. With the presidential election still several months away, the country's health is at stake[2].

1 Once darkness had fallen, the general went to see the situation for himself. Mark Milley [a four-star general] strode across the battlefield in olive-green camouflage and heavy boots, not to inspect a residential street in Fallujah or mountains in Afghanistan, but the streets of Washington, D. C. [...]

There are competing narratives[3] as to whether they [the demonstrators] had been warned before force[4] was deployed[5], but it is clear why they were moved: to provide a photo op[6] for U. S. President Donald Trump. Around 6 p. m. on Monday, after several days in which the White House had looked like a defensive fortress[7] surrounded by a sea of furious demonstrators, Trump stepped outside. Up to that point, the president had hardly said a word about the largely peaceful protests or the limited rioting that had beset[8] Washington, D. C.,

[1] **to exacerbate** to make sth. that is already bad even worse – [2] **at stake** at risk – [3] **narrative** a description of events – [4] **force** physical, esp. violent strength or power – [5] **to deploy** to move soldiers to a place where they are used – [6] **photo op** occasion when a politician or famous person is photographed doing sth. that will make thempopular with the public – [7] **fortress** *Festung*– [8] **to beset** to hurt or trouble

and dozens of other towns and cities across the nation. He was unable to find the courage or desire to give a consoling[9] speech following the horrific slaying[10] of George Floyd, a black man who was murdered by a white policeman who kneeled on his neck for almost nine minutes.

Once the crowds were cleared[11] on Monday evening, Trump stood in front of St. John's Church, which had been damaged by fire the previous evening. He fiddled[12] with a Bible, then held it aloft, as though unsure exactly what to do. When Trump was asked about his favorite verse in what he described as his "favorite book" last year, he had been unable to come up with one.

In front of the church, a journalist asked the president about his thoughts about the current situation. Trump muttered[13] a few unintelligible comments into the wind. He was surrounded exclusively by white men and women, including Defense Secretary Mark Esper and the four-star General Milley, who had been tasked by the president a short time earlier with coordinating the military response to the unrest in the country.

2 Quick Pushback

The scene was as ridiculous as it was ominous, more reminiscent[14] of South American potentates[15] than of American democracy. Trump, who is fond of talking about "my generals" and also claimed to have the "support of the army," had arranged for a military escort for his foray[16] into the streets of America. He also indicated that he wanted to send military units into American cities to confront the protesters, whom he has described as "terrorists." [...]

Trump and his political accessories[17] are using the rhetoric of authoritarianism[18]. Militarized police forces haven't just been using violence to quell[19] plundering and rioting, they have also been attacking peaceful demonstrators. Journalists have been arrested as well.

Should we be worried about the United States? Is a fundamental shift taking place in a country that is synonymous with deeply rooted democracy? The current chaos on the streets of America isn't just the product of the country's economic and societal tensions. The president himself has repeatedly exacerbated those conflicts with his rhetoric. Trump, it seems, needs the chaos. He feeds off[20] it.

Few other democratically elected leaders have as much power as the U.S. president, a reality that can lead to abuse. Trump has made personal loyalty the most important qualification for those with whom he surrounds himself. [...]

3 In the Hands of Loyal Acolytes[21]

Not long ago, it seemed absurd to question the strength of America's system of checks and balances. U.S. democracy, more than 200 years old, has survived numerous crises and its resilience[22] has always withstood attempts to grab power. But after more than three years of Trump, and despite him being the democratically elected president, the foundations of American democracy have grown brittle[23]. Trump has continually pushed back the limits of what was considered acceptable under his predecessors[24]. Flouting[25] tradition, he placed the powerful Department of the Interior and the intelligence agencies in the hands of loyal acolytes. [...]

The system of checks and balances is a long way from being defanged[26] and opposition is lively, as the streets in recent days have shown. In the House of Representatives, the Democrats have a solid majority and both Washington and New York are home to newspapers that wield[27] tremendous[28] power.

But the president is flirting with authoritarianism. And his party is following along. [...]

On Monday night, military helicopters circled at low altitude[29] above the streets of the capital to intimidate[30] demonstrators and looters[31]. In military jargon, the tactic is known as a "show of force," and tends to be used in foreign battlefields in places like Iraq and Afghanistan. Meanwhile, National Guard troops in battle equipment lined up in front of the Lincoln Memorial, their faces covered. And then, suddenly, a high fence was erected around the White House on Thursday. To protect the president from the American people. [...]

[9] **consoling** *tröstend* – [10] **slaying** a murder – [11] **to clear** to remove or get rid of whatever is blocking sth. – [12] **to fiddle** *herumfuchteln* – [13] **to mutter** *nuscheln* – [14] **reminiscent** [ˌremɪˈnɪsənt] (*fml.*) making you remember a particular person or event – [15] **potentate** *Machthaber* – [16] **foray** *Ausflug, Streifzug* – [17] **accessory** here: *Gehilfe, Komplize* – [18] **authoritarianism** the belief that people must obey completely and not be allowed freedom to act as they wish – [19] **to quell** to stop sth., esp. by using force – [20] **to feed off sth.** (*phr. v.*) to use sth. to get advantages – [21] **acolyte** (*fml.*) *Gefolgsmann* – [22] **resilience** *Widerstandsfähigkeit* – [23] **brittle** delicate and easily broken – [24] **predecessor** *Vorgänger* – [25] **to flout** to intentionally not obey a rule, law or custom – [26] **to defang** *jdn./etw. unschädlich machen* – [27] **to wield** to have a lot of influence or power – [28] **tremendous** very great in amount – [29] **altitude** height above sea level – [30] **to intimidate** *einschüchtern* – [31] **looter** *Plünderer*

4 Destructive Rioting and Curfews[32]

The U.S. has been beset by a perfect storm. In absolute numbers, no other industrialized country has been hit as hard by the coronavirus pandemic as the United States, with more than 100,000 dead. The economic consequences of the virus have also been devastating[33]: More than 40 million Americans have lost their jobs, a disaster second only to the Great Depression. And now, the killing of George Floyd has torn open the country's oldest wound: the deep-seated racism left behind by slavery.

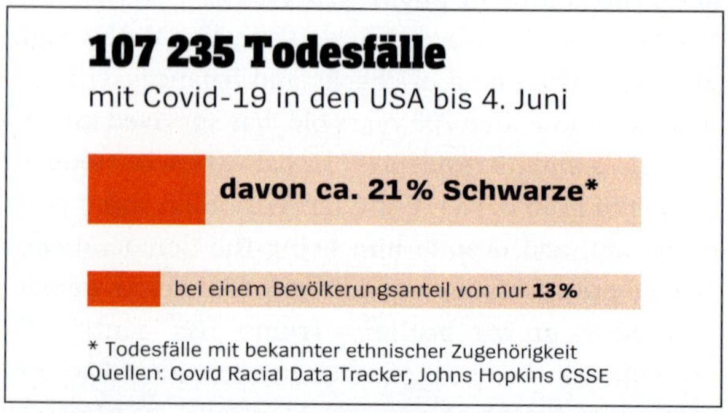

During the initial weeks of the coronavirus crisis, many people took comfort[34] in the notion[35] that "we're all in this together." The phrase was repeated daily by news anchors[36], politicians and celebrities. But many black people in the United States saw it as an affront. They have been hit much harder than white Americans by unemployment – even George Floyd had lost his job as a bouncer[37] at a restaurant in Minneapolis. Furthermore, the chance that a black American will die from COVID-19 is three times higher than for white people. [...]

When the first disturbances began following the killing of George Floyd, Trump issued a warning that culminated[38] in the sentence: "When the looting[39] starts, the shooting starts." The sentence was used in the 1960s by racist politicians and police chiefs. Trump seemed to intentionally be throwing a match into a barrel of gasoline. And now, the country is burning. [...]

5 Understanding the Rage

"No justice, no peace," is one of the most frequently chanted slogans at the demonstrations. It is often followed by a second sentence: "No racist police!" Thousands have taken to the streets of Oakland in recent days, just as they have in dozens of other cities and towns around the country: in Minneapolis, New York, Los Angeles, Dallas, Washington, Houston, Portland, Louisville and Chicago. Windows have been broken in Oakland, which is located across the bay from San Francisco, and there has been looting.

But on this recent afternoon, the protests are peaceful, at least in physical terms. The anger is still there, expressed in slogans like "fuck the police!" which is chanted[40] over and over again. The heavily armed officers, dressed in dark-colored riot gear[41], show no emotion under their helmets. [...]

"A Stab[42] in Our Hearts"

What's new, says Byers [a representative of a local civil rights organization], is that millions of Americans could see the expression on the face of the policeman Derek Chauvin as he presses his knee into the neck of George Floyd for eight minutes and 46 seconds. The video immediately went viral[43] on the internet. The lack of emotion, the impassiveness[44], says Byers, "is like a stab in our hearts." It reflects, she says, the degree of arrogance of white law enforcement officers who don't have to fear ever having to face justice for their actions. According to the Mapping Police Violence database, 99 percent of all deaths caused by police between 2013 and 2019 resulted in no charges[45] whatsoever. Each year, around 1,000 people in the United States lose their lives at the hands of the police, though the likelihood of being one of those victims is almost three times higher for blacks than it is for whites. [...]

6 Broken Out or Boarded Up

Children who grow up in Austin have a difficult start in life. "People used to think they had a chance if they worked hard and didn't give up," says Redmond [a community organizer]. But that faith is waning. "The American dream doesn't work because there is a wall: institutional racism." To show what he means, Redmond points to a large building whose windows have been bricked up. It used to be Emmet Elementary School, but like many schools in Chicago's poorer neighborhoods, the school was closed down in 2014. "The only path to advancement[46] is education," says Redmond. "There are

[32] **curfew** *Ausgangssperre* – [33] **devastating** causing a lot of damage or destruction – [34] **to take comfort in sth.** *in etw. Trost finden* – [35] **notion** belief – [36] **news anchor** sb. who is the main news reader on TV or the radio – [37] **bouncer** sb. whose job is to stand outside a bar, party, etc. and either stop people who cause trouble from coming in or force them to leave – [38] **to culminate** to be the final result of a process – [39] **looting** *das Plündern* – [40] **to chant** to repeat or sing sth. continuously – [41] **riot gear** *Kampfausrüstung* – [42] **stab** *(Dolch-) Stoß* – [43] **to go viral** to become very popular very quickly, mainly on the internet – [44] **impassiveness** *Unempfindlichkeit* – [45] **charge** (*fml.*) *Beschuldigung, Anklage* – [46] **advancement** improvement

plenty of dedicated teachers here, but there is a lack of financial means and there is a lack of desire to change things."

The American education system is heavily tilted[47] toward the haves and away from the have nots. Schools in wealthy neighborhoods receive more public funding than those in poor neighborhoods because funding is dependent on local tax revenues[48]. "Children who need help don't have a chance," Redmond says. And the many local initiatives in Austin can hardly change that situation. Now they are having to deal with the coronavirus as well. "This is a virus hotspot," says Redmond, a situation, he says, that came about in part because of high residential density[49] and a lack of quality health care. The local hospital was shut down years ago.

The virus has combined with this widespread rage to feed the current unrest on American streets. The sentence George Floyd uttered[50] as he was dying, "I can't breathe," has become the slogan of the nationwide demonstrations against police violence. But it also reflects the particularly hard impact of the COVID-19 pandemic on the black population in the past several months. [...]

7 A Question of Power

America finds itself at a high-stakes[51] crossroads. Although there has been looting and rage, hundreds of thousands of white Americans have joined the antiracist protests. Indeed, the protests seem to also be aimed at the man in the Oval Office, whose administration does not include a single black person in a prominent cabinet position and whose campaign events are almost exclusively attended by white supporters.

Outside the White House, the United States is becoming increasingly diverse[52], making it increasingly difficult to win an election without support from black and Latino voters. The unrest is thus not just about racist police officers or jobs, but about who has the say in the United States, about power. [...]

The Republicans have entered into a devil's bargain[53] with Donald Trump. He delivered all that the party has ever pined for[54]: tax cuts[55], conservative judges and sharp anti-abortion rhetoric. In return, the party has completely subordinated[56] itself to Trump, whose reelection strategy hinges on[57] the support of white voters without a college education. The strategy can only be successful if large portions of the electorate[58] are kept away from the voting booth. [...]

The Notion of American Exceptionalism[59]

American self-confidence has always been predicated[60] on the belief that it is special. In his farewell address on January 11, 1989, Ronald Reagan[61] spoke of a "shining city upon a hill," admired not only for its prosperity[62] but for its richness in ideas, its goodness and cosmopolitanism[63]. Ten months later, the Iron Curtain[64] fell, and it seemed like the age of American dominance was upon us.

This notion of American exceptionalism also came up in Trump's inauguration speech in January of 2017, al-

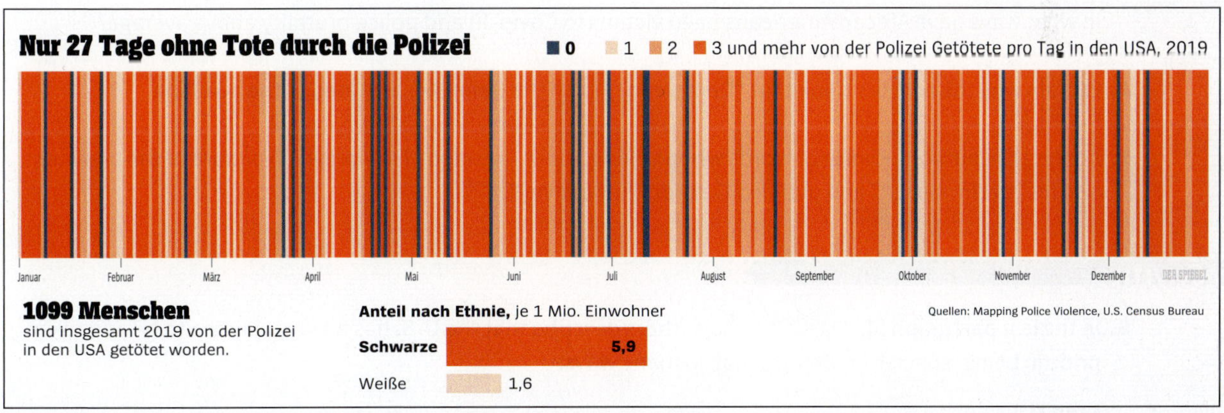

[47] **tilted** *geneigt, schräg* – [48] **tax revenue** *Steuereinkünfte* – [49] **residential density** *Bevölkerungsdichte* – [50] **to utter** (*fml.*) to say sth. – [51] **at high-stakes** involving serious risk if there is no success – [52] **diverse** [daɪˈvɜːs] including many different types of people – [53] **to enter into a devil's bargain** *sich auf einen Teufelspakt einlassen* – [54] **to pine for stb./sth** (*phr. v.*) to want or miss sb./sth. very much – [55] **tax cuts** *Steuerkürzungen* – [56] **to subordinate yourself to sb./sth.** *sich jdm. unterordnen* – [57] **to hinge on** (*phr. v.*) *von jdm./etw. abhängig sein* – [58] **electorate** all the people who are allowed to vote – [59] **exceptionalism** the idea that a person, country or political system can be allowed to be different from, and perhaps better than, others – [60] **to be predicated on** (*fml.*) to be based on – [61] **Ronald Reagan** 40th President of the US (1981 – 1989) and supporter of modern conservatism – [62] **prosperity** the state of being successful and having a lot of money – [63] **cosmopolitanism** *Weltoffenheit* – [64] **Iron Curtain** the name of the border between Western Europe and the communist countries of Eastern Europe from 1946 – 1989

albeit[65] in a vulgar form: "America will start winning again, winning like never before," the president said. Three and a half years later, there are no signs of victory. [...]

As a result, older voters in particular seem to increasingly be turning away from Trump and toward Biden and the Democrats. [...]

Now a seemingly outrageous[66] question is increasingly being asked: Would Trump accept defeat? "The next five months before the election could become very serious. Trump has the potential to significantly affect free and fair elections. [...]

SPIEGEL.DE, 05. Juni 2020; https://www.spiegel.de/international/world/a-perfect-storm-democracy-on-the-defensive-in-trump-s-america-a-00f31b18-b59e-4c45-a5f3-fde7c739d957 [06.06.2020]

COMPREHENSION

1. Read the **first paragraph** of the article (ll. 1 – 7). Point out the multiple problems the U. S. has to deal with.

2. In the following paragraphs, the authors of the article give an overview of the various problems referred to in the introductory paragraph.
   In a paired reading activity,
   - read the article on your own first,
   - summarize the contents to each other after each paragraph and clarify possible questions,
   - copy the grid below and fill in the relevant information concerning the different aspects.

President Trump's recation	African Americans	American democracy
• sending troops • ...	• ...	• ...
Trump's authoritarianism	**George Floyd**	**American dominance**
• ...	• ...	• shining city ... • ...

ANALYSIS

3. Examine the bar charts on p. 8 and p. 9:
   In what ways have African Americans been victims to Covid-19 and police brutality above average?

4. Explain why the authors think that "Democracy [is] on the Defense", as stated in the headline.

5. Analyse the authors' choice of words when talking about President Trump. Which picture of the president and his "performance" and qualifications do they convey?

ACTIVITIES

6. In the last paragraph (ll. 224 – 240), the authors describe that the U. S. has always claimed to be and taken pride in being 'special' or 'exceptional' in many ways.

   Step 1:
   In groups, collect ideas and juxtapose positive as well as negative characteristics and attitudes which you associate with "American exceptionalism".

   Step 2:
   Share and discuss your ideas in class.

[65] **albeit** [ɔːlˈbiːɪt] (*fml.*) although – [66] **outrageous** shocking and morally unacceptable

GRAMMAR / LANGUAGE

7. The authors have employed several metaphorical expressions in the article to underline their message. Turn these metaphors into everyday English to clarify their meaning:

- the country's health is at stake
- a defensive fortress surrounded by a sea of furious demonstrators
- his foray into the streets of America
- the foundations of American democracy
- the president is flirting with authoritarianism
- the killing of George Floyd has torn open the country's oldest wound
- to intentionally [throw] a match into a barrel of gasoline
- there is a wall: institutional racism
- America … at a high-stakes crossroads
- The Republicans have entered into a devil's bargain …

Tip: Use a dictionary for help if necessary.

Margaret Walker

For My People

AWARENESS

Look at the cartoon below and explain the deeper meaning of Uncle Sam's long dark shadow as depicted by cartoonist Chappatté in June 2020.

Tips on vocab

to look back ■ to look behind oneself ■ Uncle Sam ■ striped trousers ■ to wear a tailcoat (*Frack*) ■ a white goatee (*Kinnbart, Ziegenbart*) ■ stars & stripes top hat ■ to look concerned/scared ■ to cast a shadow ■ an African American man ■ to wear chains and shackles around one's neck and wrists ■ to look miserable

For my people everywhere singing their slave songs
repeatedly: their dirges[1] and their ditties[2] and their blues
and jubilees, praying their prayers nightly to an
unknown god, bending[3] their knees humbly[4] to an
unseen power;

For my people lending their strength to the years, to the
gone years and the now years and the maybe years
washing ironing cooking scrubbing sewing mending
hoeing[5] plowing digging planting pruning[6] patching[7]
dragging along never gaining never reaping[8] never
knowing and never understanding;

For my playmates in the clay and dust and sand of Alabama
backyards playing baptizing[9] and preaching and doctor
and jail and soldier and school and mama and
cooking and playhouse and concert and store and hair and
Miss Choomby[10] and company;

For the cramped[11] bewildered years we went to school to learn
to know the reasons why and the answers to and the
people who and the places where and the days when,
in memory of the bitter hours when we discovered we
were black and poor and small and different and
nobody cared and nobody wondered and nobody understood;

For the boys and girls who grew in spite of these things to be
man and woman, to laugh and dance and sing and
play and drink their wine and religion and success, to
marry their playmates and bear children and then die of
consumption[12] and anemia[13] and lynching;

For my people thronging[14] 47th Street[15] in Chicago and Lenox
Avenue[16] in New York and Rampart Street[17] in New Orleans,
lost disinherited[18] dispossessed and happy people
filling the cabarets and taverns and other people's
pockets needing bread and shoes and milk and land and
money and something – something all our own;

For my people walking blindly spreading joy, losing time
being lazy, sleeping when hungry, shouting when
burdened, drinking when hopeless, tied and shackled[19]
and tangled[20] among ourselves by the unseen creatures
who tower over[21] us omnisciently[22] and laugh;

[1] **dirge** *Trauergesang, Grabgesang* – [2] **ditty** a short simple song – [3] **to bend** *sich beugen, sich krümmen* – [4] **humble** poor or of a low social rank – [5] **to hoe** *Unkraut hacken* – [6] **to prune** *Hecken, Büsche etc. beschneiden* – [7] **to patch** *etw. flicken, reparieren* – [8] **to reap** to receive sth. as a result of your own actions – [9] **to baptize sb.** *jdn. taufen* – [10] **Miss Choomby** here: synonym for being a black woman – [11] **cramped** limited – [12] **consumption** *Tuberkulose* – [13] **anemia** *Blutarmut* – [14] **to throng** to be or go somewhere in large numbers – [15] **47th Street** known for its nightclubs where famous black artists performed – [16] **Lenox Avenue** also called Malcolm X Boulevard, the primary north-south route through Harlem – [17] **Rampart Street** the centre of an important African American commercial and entertainment district – [18] **disinherited** *enterbt* – [19] **shackled** wearing shackles; *gefesselt* – [20] **tangled** *angebunden* – [21] **to tower over sb.** (*phr. v.*) to be very tall in comparison with sb./sth. else – [22] **omnisciently** having or seeming to have unlimited knowledge

For my people blundering[23] and groping[24] and floundering[25] in
the dark of churches and schools and clubs and
societies, associations and councils and committees and
conventions, distressed[26] and disturbed and deceived and
devoured[27] by money-hungry glory-craving[28] leeches[29],
preyed on[30] by facile[31] force of state and fad[32] and
novelty[33], by false prophet and holy believer;

For my people standing staring[34] trying to fashion[35] a better
way from confusion, from hypocrisy[36] and misunderstanding,
trying to fashion a world that will hold all
the people, all the faces, all the adams and eves and
their countless generations;

Let a new earth rise. Let another world be born. Let a bloody
peace be written in the sky. Let a second generation
full of courage issue forth[37]; let a people loving freedom
come to growth. Let a beauty full of healing and a
strength of final clenching[38] be the pulsing in our
spirits and our blood. Let the martial[39] songs be
written, let the dirges disappear. Let a race of men
now rise and take control.

from *For My People* by Margaret Walker. Yale University Press (Reprint 2020), 1942, pp. 13 ff.

COMPREHENSION

Margaret Walker (1915 – 1998) was an African American poet and novelist who was born and raised in Birmingham, Alabama. *For My People*, a collection of ballad poems from which the title poem (published in 1942) is taken, was her first published book.

1. The poem is a so-called 'ballad poem', which basically means that it tells a story; in this case the poem addresses the tragic history of African American slavery.

   Step 1:
   Divide the class into six groups, with two groups working with three stanzas each (1 – 3, 4 – 6, 7 – 9).

   Step 2:
   Read the stanzas and find an appropriate title for each stanza that reflects its core topic.

   Step 3:
   Take notes on the relevant topics described in each stanza and write them on a sheet of paper.

   Step 4:
   All the groups should now attach their slips of paper chronologically to the classroom wall or blackboard.

[23] **to blunder** *herumtappen* – [24] **to grope** *herumtasten* – [25] **to flounder** *stolpern, taumeln* – [26] **distressed** upset or worried – [27] **devoured** completely eaten up – [28] **to crave** to have a very strong feeling of wanting sth. – [29] **leech** *Blutegel* – [30] **to prey on** (*phr. v.*) to kill and eat up – [31] **facile** superficial, too simple – [32] **fad** a style, activity or interest that is very popular for a short period of time – [33] **novelty** the quality of being new and unusual – [34] **to stare** to look for a long time with the eyes wide open, esp. when surprised, frightened or thinking; *starren* – [35] **to fashion** to make in a particular shape – [36] **hypocrisy** *Scheinheiligkeit* – [37] **to issue forth** to go or come out – [38] **clenching** (of teeth or fists) closing or holding tightly in a way that shows determination or anger – [39] **martial** of or suitable for war

Step 5:
In a gallery walk, read the notes you have taken, which are like a timeline of Margaret Walker's reflections on African American history as well as her own life.

Step 6:
After getting an overview of the various aspects mentioned in the poem, answer the questions below:
Which different aspects of
- slavery
- U. S. history
- the living conditions of African Americans
- the behaviour and attitude of white Americans

does the speaker of the poem describe?

ANALYSIS

2. Examine the last stanza and how it differs from the other stanzas.
   What is its message?

3. Analyse the stylistic devices the poet has employed to emphasize her appeal and the message of the poem.
   Pay particular attention to the use of:
   - alliteration and anaphora
   - repetition and parallelism
   - enumeration
   - punctuation and sentence structure

4. Only a few days after the killing of George Floyd on 25 May 2020, the renowned British street artist Banksy made a tribute to George Floyd. In addition to an artwork, he also made a statement which immediately went viral.
   a) Take a look at Banksy's artwork on p. 15 and describe its details.
      What is his message?
   b) Read Banksy's statement and explain his view.

ACTIVITIES

5. In his statement, Banksy concludes that "this is a white problem".
   Say why you do or don't share his view. Discuss in class.

GRAMMAR / LANGUAGE

@ 6. Talking about ethnicity or skin colour is a highly sensitive issue. Do research on the following terms and phrases and find out whether (or not) they are politically correct.

people of colour • ethnicity • race • Caucasian • black • white • native • indigenous • Western • coloured • African American • negro • full-blooded • multi-racial • mixed race

Banksy

George Floyd Tribute

Courtesy of Pest Control Office, Banksy, 2020

Tips on vocab

the American flag ■ Stars & Stripes ■ doves ■ to set sth. on fire ■ to light a candle in remembrance of sb. ■ a bouquet of flowers ■ tea candles

At first I thought I should just shut up and listen to black people about this issue.

But why would I do that? It is not their problem. It's mine.

People of colour are being failed by the system. The white system. Like a broken pipe flooding the apartment of the people living downstairs. This faulty system is making their life a misery, but it's not their job to fix it. They can't – no-one will let them in the apartment upstairs.

This is a white problem. And if white people don't fix it, someone will have to come upstairs and kick the door in.

https://www.instagram.com/p/CBFyA8iM15Y/?igshid=w2v2juga2emt [07.08.2020]

We the People ... Inventing Democracy

A New Idea – Government by the People

AWARENESS

In many countries today, the right to demonstrate and publicly demand changes from people such as politicians is a constitutional civil right. And even in countries where people are denied the right to publicly assemble and demonstrate, there are demonstrations and people sometimes even risk their lives to openly highlight grievances (*Missstände*).
What issues/topics do you consider important enough to demonstrate for or against? Have you ever participated in a demonstration – and what was your experience like?

The Constitution of the United States was shaped and fashioned on the forge[1] of great ideas. It is a product of a succession[2] of intellectual leaps[3] that became known as the Age of Enlightenment[4] in the eighteenth century. The German philosopher Immanuel Kant (1724–1804) defined this period in human evolution as "man's release from his self-instructed tutelage[5]," tutelage being "man's inability to make use of his understanding without direction from another."
The English-born American émigré and firebrand[6] journalist Thomas Paine (1737–1809) called it the Age of Reason[7]. At a time when the ability to rule men's lives lay in the divine right of kings, where monarchical decree[8] controlled life, death, liberty, and freedom of speech, and birthright condemned[9] the rise of a person regardless of his or her ability, some men of letters turned their thoughts to the question "Why?".
Government managed by the ancient Greeks' democracy, or the Romans' republic – with the power of the citizens' vote, or political representation of the citizens' need – had long been suppressed. But the printed and published words of those referred to in their time as the "substitute aristocracy" – learned man such as John Jacques Rousseau (1712–1778), "I prefer liberty with danger than peace with slavery," or John Locke (1632–1704), "Being all equal and independent, no one ought to harm another in his life, health, liberty, or possessions" – gained acceptance during a period when people believed they were oppressed.

Isolated from the Old World's tyranny, the American colonies felt cut off from representation by their mother country, Great Britain. The colonists had come to this wild and vast new world on the east coast of North America and had worked hard to support themselves and become valuable trading partners as loyal subjects of their king. British acts against Americans' liberty and levies[10] against commerce were becoming intolerable. As treasonous[11] threats[12] and autocratic demands sailed back and forth between American and English ports, new ideas and enlightened thoughts were being born in the salons and cafés of Europe. These entitlements[13] spoke of the people's inalienable[14] rights and representational government shaped by their own hands.
Provocations and demands on the colonies such as the Stamp Act[15], the Townshend Acts[16], and boarding British troops in private Boston homes demanded an immediate declaration of independence in 1775. A more moderate group, led by John Dickinson of Pennsylvania, appealed for a final letter to be extended[17] directly to the Crown seeking a peaceful solution. This so-called Olive Branch Petition placed all the guilt on Parliament, which the colonies presumed[18] had acted without the king's knowledge. George III refused to accept it. He called down[19] the wrath[20] of the empire on every colonist who dared sign such a document.
On November 9, 1775, three months after the Olive Branch Petition had been rejected and every signatory branded traitor with a reward on their heads, the Con-

[1] **forge** *Schmiede(feuer)* – [2] **succession** *Abfolge* – [3] **leap** here: a big change, increase or improvement – [4] **Age of Enlightenment** *das Zeitalter der Aufklärung* – [5] **tutelage** *Unmündigkeit* – [6] **firebrand** *Aufwiegler* – [7] **Age of Reason** *das Zeitalter der Vernunft* – [8] **decree** official statement that sth. must happen – [9] **to condemn** here: *verhindern* – [10] **levy** *Abgabe, Gebühr* – [11] **treasonous** *hochverräterisch* – [12] **threat** [θret] *Drohung* – [13] **entitlement** the right to do or have sth. – [14] **inalienable** unable to be removed; *unveräußerlich* – [15] **Stamp Act** a tax imposed on printed material produced in the colonies – [16] **Townshend Act** a series of British acts of Parliament imposed on the colonies – [17] **to extend** here (*fml.*): to give sth. to sb. – [18] **to presume** *vermuten* – [19] **to call down sth. (on sb.)** *jdm. mit etw. drohen* – [20] **wrath** extreme anger

tinental Congress created and agreement of secrecy to protect these fugitives[21] from the death penalty. It was eventually signed by eighty-seven delegates.

With all diplomatic channels exhausted, all that remained was separation from the mother country and the turning of thirteen colonies into independent states. This decision almost certainly meant going to war with the greatest military power in Western civilizations. To earn support from the majority of citizens in this shaky new republic would require a lot of explaining. A formal declaration stating the reasons for such a drastic step was deemed[22] a necessity. [...]

On May 15, 1776, Richard Henry Lee, a delegate from Virginia, received instructions to approve separation and the severing[23] of all ties with Britain. In response, he placed the following resolution before Congress:

Resolved, that these United Colonies are, and of right ought to be, free and independent States, that they are absolved from all allegiance[24] to the British Crown, and that all political connection between them and the State of Great Britain is, and ought to be, totally dissolved.

The resolution was roundly debated, but also aced[25] as motivation to produce a necessary explanation of why the colonies were to become independent states. [...] Once a general outline was established, Jefferson was persuaded to write the first draft, which he did, working on the second floor of a boarding house using a portable writing desk he designed and built. [...]

On July 4, 1776, the final form of the document was approved with the signatures of fifty-six delegates – all of whom faced hanging if arrested by the British for doing so. It was then sent to the printers to be distributed and read throughout the newly minted[26] United States of America.

from *The Constitution* by Gerry Souter, Janet Souter. Carlton Books Ltd., London 2019, pp. 8 ff.

1

George Washington and the US Constitution; painting by Junius Brutus Stearns, 1856

COMPREHENSION

1. In a **first reading**, try to understand the **gist** of the text.

2. Exchange your first understanding of the text with a partner and clarify possible questions.

[21] **fugitive** *Flüchtling* – [22] **to deem** (*fml.*) to consider sth. in a particular way – [23] **to sever** to end a connection with sb./sth., esp. by cutting – [24] **allegiance** [ə'liːdʒəns] (*fml.*) loyalty and support for a ruler, country, group or belief – [25] **to ace** (*infml.*) to do sth. very well – [26] **to mint** to produce or invent sth. new; *prägen*

3. Now, read the text a second time and try to complete the sentences below by using or referring to evidence from the text:
a) German philosopher Immanuel Kant defined the Age of Enlightenment as ...
b) Jean Jacques Rousseau thought that ...
c) John Locke demanded that ...
d) The American colonists were very self-confident because ...
e) British provocations of the colonists were ...
f) George III's reaction to the Olive Branch Petition was ...
g) The signatories of the Olive Branch Petition were considered ...
h) The reasons for a formal declaration were ...
i) The general outline of Lee's resolution was to ...

4. Take a close at the painting (no. 1) on p. 17 depicting the delegates participating in the Constitutional Convention.
- What overall atmosphere does the painting convey of the Convention?
- What impression is revealed of the participating delegates?
- What kind of men/politicians do they appear to be?

ANALYSIS

5. Although the text's diction and overall tone appears to be matter-of-fact and neutral, the American colonists and Founding Fathers of the nation are presented in a certain light.
Find examples in the text that present them as true democrats and brave and honest patriots.

ACTIVITIES

6. The author states that going to war with Britain "require[d] a lot of explaining" to "earn support from the majority of the citizens" (ll. 67 ff.).
Imagine you were one of the delegates: What would you tell the colonists to convince them to separate from and fight against the greatest (military) power of its time, the British Empire?
In a group, develop ideas and compile a short pamphlet to justify your revolutionary ideas.

2

DEALERS INSPECTING A NEGRO AT A SLAVE AUCTION IN VIRGINIA. – FROM A SKETCH BY OUR SPECIAL ARTIST.

7. However noble and democratic the American Founding Fathers may have been, forty of the fifty-six delegates who signed the Declaration of Independence were slave owners.

Step 1: Look at the woodcut (no. 2), which shows a slave auction in Virginia. What impression does it convey of a) the white slave owners and traders, and b) the slave who is being examined?

Step 2: Using the weblinks below to help you, research the history and development of slavery in the United States in the 18th and 19th centuries.
- https://www.history.com/topics/black-history/slavery
- https://www.theguardian.com/news/2019/aug/15/400-years-since-slavery-timeline
- https://www.nationalgeographic.org/interactive/slavery-united-states/
- https://www.britannica.com/topic/African-American/Slavery-in-the-United-States

The Declaration of Independence

AWARENESS

After the founding of the first British trading post in Jamestown, Virginia, in 1607, the settlements in the 'New World' kept growing and thriving. The establishment of the Atlantic Triangle Trade was a perfect tool to move and exchange goods and slaves, thus enabling the rise of the British Empire and the Industrial Revolution. To put it in a nutshell: the British colonies in America were a real success story.

Against this background, what do you consider to be the reasons why the colonists risked being killed, why they turned against their mother country and why they even went to war in order to become an independent nation? Discuss in class.

1 In Congress, July 4, 1776.

The unanimous[1] Declaration of the thirteen united States of America,

When in the Course of human events, it becomes necessary for one people to dissolve the political bands which have connected them with another, and to assume among the powers of the earth, the separate and equal station to which the Laws of Nature and of Nature's God entitle them, a decent respect to the opinions of mankind requires that they should declare the causes which impel[2] them to the separation.

We hold these truths to be self-evident, that all men are created equal, that they are endowed[3] by their Creator with certain unalienable Rights, that among these are Life, Liberty and the pursuit of Happiness. – That to secure these rights, Governments are instituted among Men, deriving[4] their just powers from the consent of the governed, – That whenever any Form of Government becomes destructive of these ends, it is the Right of the People to alter or to abolish it, and to institute new Government, laying its foundation on such principles and organizing its powers in such form, as to them shall seem most likely to effect their Safety and Happiness.

2 Prudence[5] indeed, will dictate that Governments long established should not be changed for light and transient[6] causes; and accordingly all experience hath shewn[7], that mankind are more disposed[8] to suffer, while evils are sufferable, than to right themselves by abolishing the forms to which they are accustomed[9]. But when a long train of abuses and usurpations[10], pursuing invariably the same Object evinces[11] a design to reduce them under absolute Despotism[12], it is their right, it is their duty, to throw off such Government, and to provide new Guards for their future security. – Such has been the patient sufferance of these Colonies; and such is now the necessity which constrains[13] them to alter their former Systems of Government. The history of the present King of Great Britain is a history of repeated injuries and usurpations, all having in direct object the establishment of an absolute Tyranny over these States. To prove this, let Facts be submitted to a candid[14] world.

3
- He has refused his Assent[15] to Laws, the most wholesome and necessary for the public good.
- He has forbidden his Governors to pass Laws of immediate and pressing importance, unless suspended[16] in their operation till his Assent should be obtained[17]; and when so suspended, he has utterly neglected to attend to them.
- He has refused to pass other Laws for the accommodation[18] of large districts of people, unless those people would relinquish[19] the right of Representation in the Legislature, a right inestimable[20] to them and formidable[21] to tyrants only.
- He has called together legislative bodies at places unusual, uncomfortable, and distant from the depository[22] of their public Records, for the sole purpose of fatiguing[23] them into compliance[24] with his measures.
- He has dissolved Representative Houses repeatedly, for opposing with manly firmness his invasions on the rights of the people.

[1] **unanimous** supported or agreed by everyone. – [2] **to impel** to force sb. to take action. – [3] **to be endowed with sth.** to have sth. from birth – [4] **to derive sth. from** to get sth. – [5] **prudence** behaviour that is careful and avoids risks – [6] **transient** temporary – [7] **shewn** (*old use*) shown – [8] **disposed** (*fml.*) willing or likely to do sth. – [9] **accustomed** familiar with sth. – [10] **usurpation** *widerrechtliche Aneignung* – [11] **to evince** (*fml.*) to show clearly – [12] **despotism** *Willkürherrschaft* – [13] **to constrain** to force into an unwanted action – [14] **candid** honest and telling the truth – [15] **assent** official approval; *Zustimmung* – [16] **to suspend** to stop sth. from being active – [17] **to obtain** to get – [18] **accommodation** *Versorgung* – [19] **to relinquish** to give up – [20] **inestimable** immeasurable; *unschätzbar* – [21] **formidable** frightening – [22] **depository** *Aufbewahrungsort* – [23] **to fatigue** to make sb. extremely tired – [24] **compliance** the act of obeying an order or rule

- He has refused for a long time, after such dissolutions, to cause others to be elected; whereby the Legislative powers, incapable of Annihilation[25], have returned to the People at large for their exercise; the State remaining in the mean time exposed to all the dangers of invasion from without, and convulsions[26] within.
- He has endeavoured[27] to prevent the population of these States; for that purpose obstructing[28] the Laws of Naturalization of Foreigners; refusing to pass others to encourage their migrations hither, and raising the conditions of new Appropriations[29] of Lands.
- He has obstructed the Administration of Justice, by refusing his Assent to Laws for establishing Judiciary powers.
- He has made Judges dependent on his Will alone, for the tenure[30] of their offices, and the amount and payment of their salaries.
- He has erected a multitude of New Offices, and sent hither swarms of Officers to harass[31] our people, and eat out their substance.
- He has kept among us, in times of peace, Standing Armies without the Consent of our legislatures.
- He has affected to render[32] the Military independent of and superior to the Civil power.
- He has combined with others to subject us to a jurisdiction foreign to our constitution, and unacknowledged by our laws; giving his Assent to their Acts of pretended Legislation:
  - For Quartering large bodies of armed troops among us:
  - For protecting them, by a mock Trial, from punishment for any Murders which they should commit on the Inhabitants of these States:
  - For cutting off our Trade with all parts of the world:
  - For imposing[33] Taxes on us without our Consent:
  - For depriving[34] us in many cases, of the benefits of Trial by Jury:
  - For transporting us beyond Seas to be tried for pretended offences
  - For abolishing the free System of English Laws in a neighbouring Province, establishing therein an Arbitrary[35] government, and enlarging its Boundaries so as to render it at once an example and fit instrument for introducing the same absolute rule into these Colonies:
  - For taking away our Charters, abolishing our most valuable Laws, and altering fundamentally the Forms of our Governments:
  - For suspending our own Legislatures, and declaring themselves invested with power to legislate for us in all cases whatsoever.
- He has abdicated[36] Government here, by declaring us out of his Protection and waging[37] War against us.
- He has plundered our seas, ravaged[38] our Coasts, burnt our towns, and destroyed the lives of our people.
- He is at this time transporting large Armies of foreign Mercenaries[39] to compleat the works of death, desolation and tyranny, already begun with circumstances of Cruelty & perfidy[40] scarcely paralleled in the most barbarous ages, and totally unworthy the Head of a civilized nation.
- He has constrained[41] our fellow Citizens taken Captive on the high Seas to bear Arms against their Country, to become the executioners of their friends and Brethren[42], or to fall themselves by their Hands.
- He has excited[43] domestic insurrections[44] amongst us, and has endeavoured to bring on[45] the inhabitants of our frontiers, the merciless Indian Savages, whose known rule of warfare, is an undistinguished destruction of all ages, sexes and conditions.

4 In every stage of these Oppressions We have Petitioned for Redress[46] in the most humble[47] terms: Our repeated Petitions have been answered only by repeated injury. A Prince whose character is thus marked by every act which may define a Tyrant, is unfit to be the ruler of a free people.

Nor have We been wanting in attentions to our British brethren. We have warned them from time to time of attempts by their legislature to extend an unwarrantable[48] jurisdiction over us. We have reminded them of the circumstances of our emigration and settlement here. We have appealed to their native justice and mag-

[25] **annihilation** *Aufhebung* – [26] **convulsion** *Erschütterung* – [27] **to endeavour** to try to do sth. – [28] **to obstruct** *blockieren* – [29] **appropriation** *Besitzergreifung, Bereitstellung* – [30] **tenure** the time period in which sb. hold an important job – [31] **to harass** to continue to annoy or upset sb. – [32] **to render** to make – [33] **to impose** *auferlegen, aufbürden* – [34] **to deprive sb. of sth.** to take sth. away from sb. – [35] **arbitrary** *willkürlich* – [36] **to abdicate** to give up officially – [37] **to wage** to fight a war – [38] **to ravage** to cause great damage to sth. – [39] **mercenary** *Söldner* – [40] **perfidy** behaviour that is not loyal – [41] **to constrain** to control and limit sth. – [42] **brethren** brothers – [43] **to excite** to provoke; *jdn. anstacheln* – [44] **insurrection** rebellion – [45] **to bring on** here: *aufwiegeln* - [46] **redress** (*fml.*) *Abhilfe* – [47] **humble** *demütig* – [48] **unwarrantable** *ungerechtfertigt*

nanimity[49], and we have conjured[50] them by the ties of our common kindred to disavow[51] these usurpations, which, would inevitably interrupt our connections and correspondence. They too have been deaf to the voice of justice and of consanguinity[52]. We must, therefore, acquiesce[53] in the necessity, which denounces[54] our Separation, and hold them, as we hold the rest of mankind, Enemies in War, in Peace Friends.

5 We, therefore, the Representatives of the united States of America, in General Congress, Assembled, appealing to the Supreme Judge of the world for the rectitude[55] of our intentions, do, in the Name, and by Authority of the good People of these Colonies, solemnly publish and declare, That these United Colonies are, and of Right ought to be Free and Independent States; that they are Absolved from all Allegiance[56] to the British Crown, and that all political connection between them and the State of Great Britain, is and ought to be totally dissolved; and that as Free and Independent States, they have full Power to levy[57] War, conclude Peace, contract Alliances, establish Commerce, and to do all other Acts and Things which Independent States may of right do. And for the support of this Declaration, with a firm reliance on the protection of divine[58] Providence[59], we mutually[60] pledge to each other our Lives, our Fortunes and our sacred Honor.

https://www.archives.gov/founding-docs/declaration-transcript [06.06.2020]

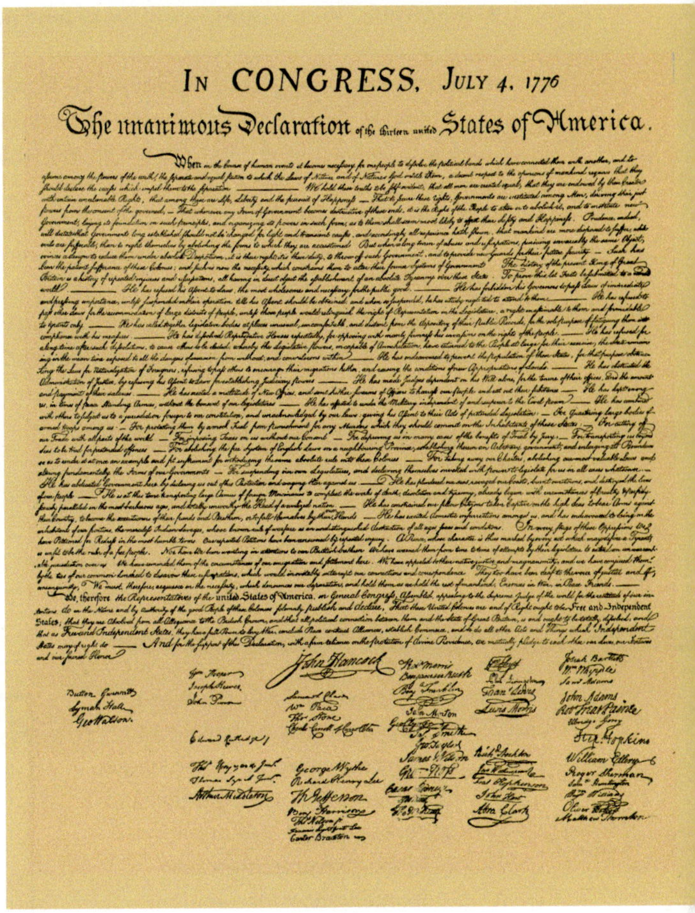

The handwritten declaration signed by the fifty-six delegates

COMPREHENSION

When, in the 1750s, the American colonists refused to pay taxes and rebelled against the British crown, they were considered to be and treated as terrorists and traitors who had committed the crime of treason and therefore faced the death penalty and execution.
In the Declaration, which Thomas Jefferson wrote in 1776, the colonies aim at justifying their reasons for taking such drastic action. Whereas only a few of the most famous lines of the Declaration of Independence are usually cited, the text on pp. 19 ff. is the complete document, which can be subdivided into several thematic units.

1. In a **first reading**, get an overview of the different parts of the declaration and what they are about. Then, together with a partner, find an appropriate sub-heading for each part.

2. The **first part** is one of the most famous and most frequently quoted texts in history. Point out
   - the reasons given here for writing the declaration
   - the inalienable rights given to men
   - the reasons given for wanting to abolish and change a government.

[49] **magnanimity** (*fml.*) kindness and generosity – [50] **to conjure** here: to request solemnly – [51] **to disavow** (*fml.*) here: to give up – [52] **consanguinity** (*fml.*) the condition of being blood relations – [53] **to acquiesce in sth.** (*fml.*) to accept sth. unwillingly – [54] **to denounce** to criticize sb. strongly and publicly – [55] **rectitude** honesty and correct moral behaviour – [56] **allegiance** loyalty and support for a ruler – [57] **to levy** to make or begin war – [58] **divine** *göttlich* – [59] **providence** *Vorsehung* – [60] **mutually** *gegenseitig*

3. Which other reasons are given in the **second part** that explain and justify the separation from Great Britain?

4. The **third and longest part** presents 27 accusations against the British king, George III.
Outline the described misdemeanours (*Fehlverhalten*) and point out which fields of government they belong to, e.g. legislation, economy, trade, immigration, administration.

5. The **fourth part** offers further explanations of the colonists' demands and the king's responses.
Jot down the most relevant information given here.

6. The **concluding fifth part** of the declaration presents the colonists' declaration.
State what precisely the colonists declare and how they plan their future.

ANALYSIS

7. Examine the structure of the declaration and explain the function and effect of specific rhetorical devices, e.g.
   - the line of argument,
   - climax,
   - repetition,
   - the use of personal pronouns.

ACTIVITIES

8. Do a project on the Declaration of Independence, its author and the historical circumstances of its origin. You may want to use the weblinks below to get further information.
   - https://www.archives.gov/founding-docs/declaration-transcript
   - https://www.archives.gov/founding-docs
   - https://www.monticello.org/thomas-jefferson/jefferson-s-three-greatest-achievements/the-declaration/transcript-of-the-rough-of-the-declaration
   - https://www.monticello.org

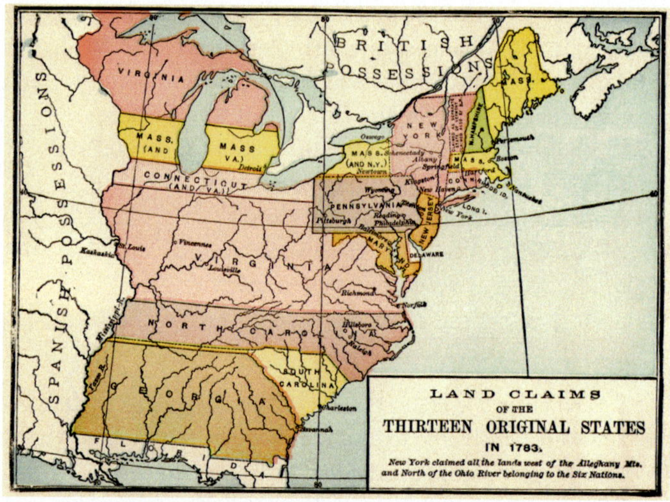

The first thirteen colonies and states of the United States

9. In the run-up to the rebellion and the drafting of the Declaration of Independence, there were endless discussions and debates about whether (or not) separating from Great Britain would be the right thing to do.
Act out a panel discussion in which you present and discuss the different pros and cons, views and possible problems to be expected.

10. As revolutionary and iconic as this declaration may have been, it cannot be denied that it excluded hundreds of thousands of people and withheld basic human rights from women, Native Americans and African Americans.
What do you consider to be the reason why only 'white male' citizens were the beneficiaries of the new democratic rules?
Discuss in class.

The Constitution of the United States

AWARENESS

While the *Declaration of Independence* focuses on human rights and the announcement of freedom from British rule, the U. S. Constitution, ratified in 1788, guarantees the protection of individual civil rights. After a few years the Constitution was expanded by ten amendments which describe basic rights like freedom of speech, religion, the press and the right to assemble. These permanent additions, called the *Bill of Rights*, were ratified in 1791. However, more additions to the Constitution were deemed necessary over time, such as e. g. the 13th, 14th and 15th amendments in 1865, 1868 and 1870.

Against the background of your knowledge of politics from your history or social science classes, what do you consider to be the most relevant civil rights and regulations that have to be included in a country's constitution?

Preamble to the Constitution

"We the People of the United States, in Order to form a more perfect Union, establish Justice, insure domestic Tranquility[1], provide for the common defense, promote the general Welfare, and secure the Blessings of Liberty to ourselves and our Posterity[2], do ordain[3] and establish this Constitution for the United States of America."

Article II – The President

Section 1

The Executive Power shall be vested[4] in a President of the United States of America. He shall hold his Office during the Term of four Years, and together with the Vice President, chosen for the same Term, be elected as follows: [...]

In Case of the Removal of the President from Office, or of his Death, Resignation, or Inability to discharge[5] the Powers and Duties of the said Office, the Same shall devolve[6] on the Vice President, and the Congress may by Law provide for the Case of Removal, Death, Resignation or Inability, both of the President and Vice President, declaring what Officer shall then act as President, and such Officer shall act accordingly, until the Disability is removed, or a President shall be re-elected. [...]

Before [the President] enters on the Execution of his Office, he shall take the following Oath or Affirmation – "I do solemnly swear (or affirm) that I will faithfully execute the Office of President of the United States, and will to the best of my Ability, preserve, protect and defend the Constitution of the United States."

Section 2

The President shall be Commander in Chief of the Army and Navy of the United States, and of the Militia of the Several States [...]

He shall have Power, by and with the Advice and Consent of the Senate, to make Treaties, provided two thirds of the Senators present concur[7]; and he shall nominate, and by and with the Advice and Consent of the Senate,

[1] **tranquility** a peaceful, calm state without violence or worry – [2] **posterity** (*fml.*) the people who will exist in the future; *Nachkommen* – [3] **to ordain** *anordnen, verfügen* – [4] **to vest** to give sb. the power to do sth. – [5] **to discharge** to perform a duty or promise properly – [6] **to devolve on** to pass on power or responsibility to sb. at a lower level – [7] **to concur** (*fml.*) to agree or have the same opinion

shall appoint Ambassadors, other public Ministers and Consuls, Judges of the Supreme Court, and all other Officers of the United States [...]

Section 3

He shall from time to time give to the Congress Information on the State of the Union, and recommend to their Consideration such Measures as he shall judge necessary and expedient[8]; [...]

Section 4

The President, Vice President and all Civil Officers of the United States, shall be removed from Office on Impeachment[9] for, and Conviction of, Treason, Bribery, or other high Crimes and Misdemeanors[10].

Amendments to the Constitution

13th Amendment to the Constitution

Section 1. Neither slavery nor involuntary servitude, except as a punishment for crime whereof the party shall have been duly convicted, shall exist within the United States, or any place subject to their jurisdiction. (Adopted on December 6, 1865)

14th Amendment to the Constitution

Section 1. All persons born or naturalized[11] in the United States, and subject to the jurisdiction thereof, are citizens of the United States and of the State wherein they reside. No State shall make or enforce any law which shall abridge[12] the privileges or immunities[13] of citizens of the United States; nor shall any State deprive any person of life, liberty, or property, without due process of law; nor deny to any person within its jurisdiction the equal protection of the laws. (Adopted on July 9, 1868)

15th Amendment to the Constitution

Section 1. The right of citizens of the United States to vote shall not be denied or abridged by the United States or by any State on account of race, color, or previous condition of servitude[14]. (Adopted on February 3, 1870)

https://billofrightsinstitute.org/founding-documents/bill-of-rights/ [07.08.2020]

COMPREHENSION

1. What does the *Preamble to the Constitution* reveal about the intention of its authors?

2. The President of the United States has more power than most democratically elected political leaders worldwide. Therefore, it is important to regulate precisely his rights and duties.
   Read the excerpts from Article II and point out what is said about
   - the power of the president
   - the term of office
   - regulations concerning the removal or replacement of the president
   - the oath of office
   - the president's duties in relation to Congress.

3. The 13th, 14th and 15th Amendments to the Constitution were added after the Civil War (1861 – 1865) and the abolition of slavery.
   - Which further (civil) rights do these amendments guarantee to the people?
   - Who are the 'beneficiaries' (*Nutznießer*) of these amendments?

[8] **expedient** useful for a purpose – [9] **impeachment** the act of making a formal statement that a public official might be guilty of a serious offence in connection with their job, especially in the U. S.; *Amtsenthebungsverfahren* – [10] **misdemeanour** an action that is considered bad or breaks a rule but is not a crime; *Fehlverhalten* – [11] **to naturalize** to make sb. a legal citizen of a country that they were not born in – [12] **to abridge** to reduce sb.'s freedom, rights, etc. – [13] **immunity** a situation in which you are protected from legal action – [14] **servitude** (*fml.*) the state of being under the control of sb. else and having no freedom; slavery

ANALYSIS

4. Examine the wording of the presidential oath of office, which requires the president to "preserve, protect and defend the Constitution of the United States". At first sight, this seems to be quite abstract. Looking at it more practically, this oath demands immense responsibility of American president.
In a group, do further research on this document, using the weblinks below, and collect ideas about the comprehensive (*umfassend*) responsibilities and duties of the U.S. President.
- https://billofrightsinstitute.org/founding-documents/bill-of-rights/
- https://en.wikipedia.org/wiki/United_States_Bill_of_Rights
- https://www.archives.gov/founding-docs/bill-of-rights-transcript

ACTIVITIES

5. Take a closer look at the choice of words used in the Preamble:
"We the People … for the common defence … for the general welfare … to ourselves and our posterity …"

The use of specific pronouns and adjectives raises certain expectations in the reader. Given the historical context of the document – discuss the addressees of the document: who is meant by "we"?

6. Article II, section 1 states that "in case of … Inability" the president and vice-president are to be removed from office and "discharged" of their powers and duties.
- Judging from your point of view, what makes a politician or political leader well-suited or unfit for office?
- What political and personal qualifications do you expect a politician or political leader to have?

Discuss in class.

We the People ... Fighting Injustice

AWARENESS

Step 1:
Describe the cartoon below which depicts a special version of the famous Stars & Stripes/U. S. flag.

Step 2:
The caption of the cartoon, *From Sea to Shining Sea*, is a line from one of the most popular and patriotic U. S. songs, *America the Beautiful*, which was published in 1892.
@ Do research on the song (https://en.wikipedia.org/wiki/America_the_Beautiful) and find out about the lyrics of the 1911 version and their message.

Step 3:
Against the background of the passion and patriotism expressed in the song, explain the implied meaning of the cartoon and the message it wants to convey.

FROM SEA TO SHINING SEA

Tips on vocab
the U. S. flag ■ Stars & Stripes ■ billowing red and white flames ■ white hoods (of the Ku Klux Klan) against a blue ground ■ to set sth. on fire ■ to go up in flames

If One Really Wishes to Know ...

Well, if one really wishes to know how justice is administered[1] in a country, one does not question the policemen, the lawyers, the judges, or the protected members of the middle class. One goes to the unprotected – those, precisely, who need the law's protection most! – and listens to their testimony[2]. Ask any Mexican, any Puerto Rican, any black man, any poor person – ask the wretched[3] how they fare[4] in the halls of justice, and then you will know, not whether or not the country is just, but whether or not it has any love for justice, or any concept of it. It is certain, in any case, that ignorance, allied[5] with power, is the most ferocious[6] enemy justice can have.

from *No Name in the Street* by James Baldwin. Vintage Books. New York 2007, p. 149

[1] **to administer** to give sth. to sb. – [2] **testimony** (*fml.*) spoken or written statements that sth. is true – [3] **wretched** unhappy, poor – [4] **to fare** (*old use*) to succeed or be treated in the stated way – [5] **to ally with sth.** *sich mit etw. vereinigen* – [6] **ferocious** [fəˈrəʊʃəs] frightening and violent

Zellie Rainey Orr

America

[As we near the celebration of our nation's independence this July 4, 2014, I have attached a poem I penned[1] in the late 1960's while a student at Gentry High (Indianola, MS). Now nearly 50 years later, in revisiting the verbiage[2] – I concur[3] there has been progress. Yet, we still have a long way to go!!! – Zellie Rainey Orr.]

I have believed in America
though she has never believed in me;
she enslaved my ancestors
in her Land of Liberty.

She used me in building America
but refused to give me pay;
even manipulated justice
to look the other way.

She gave me an education
second-rate at that;
and blames me for illiteracy[4],
poverty, and rats.

She threw me in her crowded jails
even beat me unmercifully[5];
when I stood up for my civil rights
and protested peacefully.

She brainwashed my mind –
destroyed my self-esteem;
denied me my God-given right
to be the best, I can be.

I see her flag of freedom
flying majestically for all to see;
but I know her stars and stripes
do not wave to me.

https://www.crmvet.org/poetry/pzellie.htm [12.10.2020], "Journal of Poetry" by Zellie Rainey Orr. Penned late 1960's, 2001

COMPREHENSION

James Baldwin (1924 – 1987) was an African American novelist, playwright, poet and civil rights activist. Disillusioned by American prejudice against African Americans, he left the U. S. at the age of 24 and spent most of his life in France.

Zellie Rainey Orr (*1951) is an African American poet, historian and author who was one of the first five black students to attend the then segregated Indianola High School in Mississippi in 1957.

1. Outline Baldwin's reflections on a country's and its officials' attitude to and handling of justice.

2. Read **Zellie Rainey Orr's** poem and find keywords or lines that can be related to the statements below.

   Note: There are more aspects listed than can be found in the poem.

   a) Some of the core American beliefs and values are the pride in being American, liberty, equality and the right to live a secure life.
   b) Basic human rights like 'Life, Liberty and the Pursuit of Happiness' are important to the United States.
   c) The Atlantic triangle trade was the source of Britain's wealth and success.
   d) Slavery was the foundation of the wealth of the American southern states.
   e) The Puritans believed that hard work, discipline and self-improvement lead to success and prosperity.

[1] **to pen sth.** (*fml.*) to write sth. – [2] **verbiage** (*fml., disapproving*) language that is over-complicated and contains a lot of unnecessary words; *Wortschwall* – [3] **to concur** (*fml.*) to agree or have the same opinion – [4] **illiteracy** the lack of the ability to read or write – [5] **unmercifully** *unbarmherzig, mitleidslos*

f) The so-called 'Black Codes' denied southern Blacks the right to vote, the right to own land and excluded them from certain jobs.
g) The American South strictly enforced segregation.
h) The 1880s – 1920s were the peak years of lynching.
i) In 1870, the Fifteenth Amendment guaranteed Blacks the right to vote but the states demanded literacy tests.
j) At the March on Washington, 250,000 people listened to Martin Luther King's famous speech "I have a dream".

ANALYSIS

3. Explain James Baldwin's conclusion that "ignorance, allied with power, is the most ferocious enemy justice can have".

4. Relate the last stanza of Zellie Rainey Orr's poem to the cartoon of the U. S. flag on p. 26. Which "Stars & Stripes" wave for African Americans?

5. In 1863, Abraham Lincoln signed the *Emancipation Proclamation*, which officially abolished slavery and paved the way for the Thirteenth Amendment to the Constitution, which abolished slavery by law in 1865. Against your results from task 3, describe the cartoon below and explain what Abraham Lincoln thinks about the country's 'worst enemy'.

Tips on vocab

the Lincoln Memorial in Washington D. C. ■ Lincoln sitting on a pedestal and a throne-like armchair ■ a wall daubed with slogans ■ splashes of paint ■ to look weary/exhausted ■ to be aghast (*bestürzt sein, sich an den Kopf fassen*)

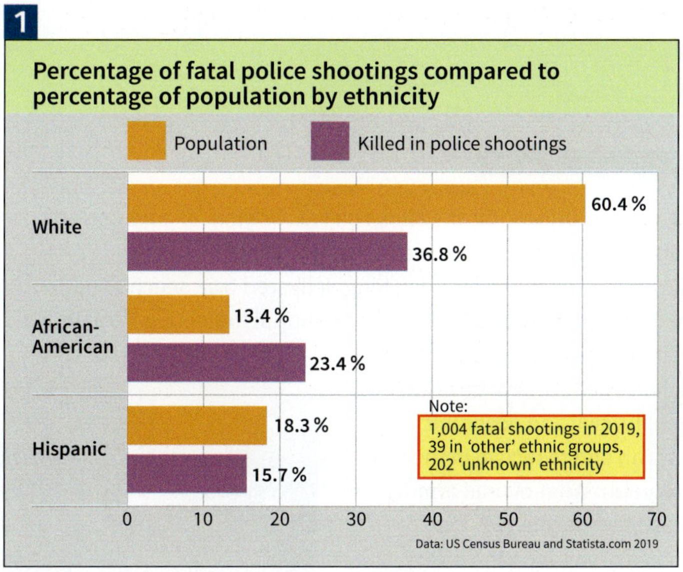

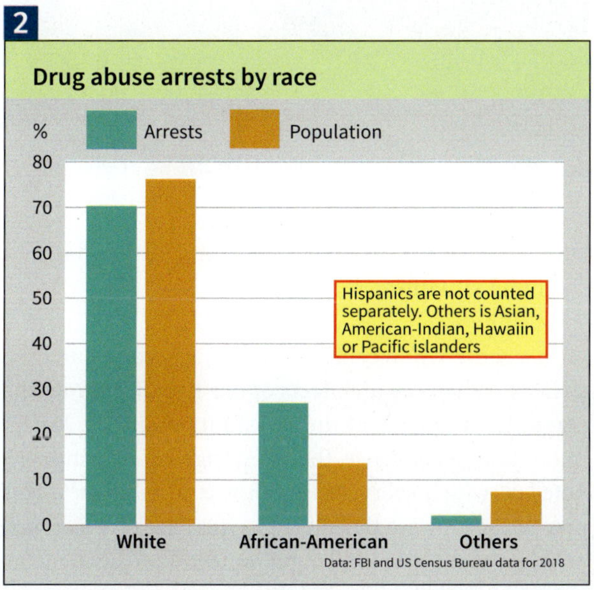

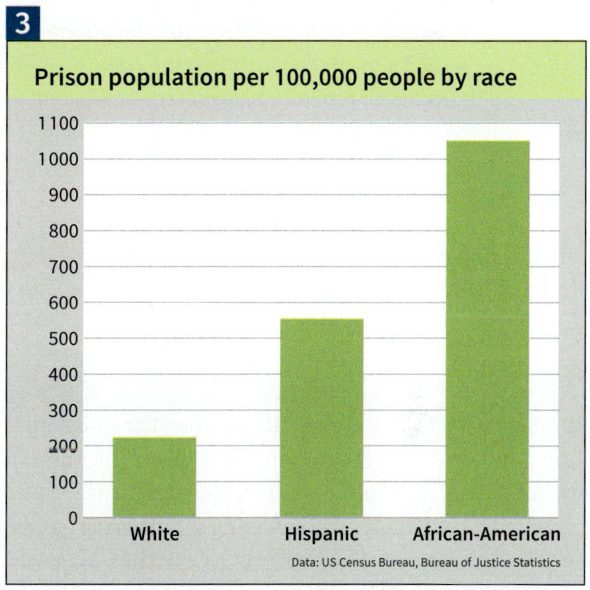

Tips on vocab

to be disproportionately higher/lower than ▪ twice as much/many ▪ in comparison to ▪ to show a significant difference in

6. Examine the bar charts above. How are African Americans and Hispanics disproportionately affected by and involved in shootings, arrests and imprisonment? What do you consider to be the possible reasons?

ACTIVITIES

7. In her introduction to the poem, Zellie Rainey Orr states that "there has been progress".
Against the background of the many problems mentioned in the poem and your knowledge of the United States, do you agree with her that there have been improvements for African Americans?
Discuss in class.

Martin Luther King Jr.

I Have a Dream

AWARENESS

On 28 August 1963, Martin Luther King Jr.'s *March on Washington for Jobs and Freedom* culminated in one of the most famous speeches in U. S. history, *I Have a Dream*.

On the steps leading to the Lincoln Memorial, King delivered his speech to more than 250,000 civil rights supporters who had gathered around the Lincoln Memorial Reflecting Pool, located on the National Mall, between the Washington Monument and the Lincoln Memorial. In his speech, Martin Luther King called for equality, civil and economic rights for blacks and an end to racism in the U.S.

a) Study the photograph: What overall atmosphere of the event does it convey?

b) Why was the choice of this location a very smart idea?

c) From today's perspective, what location would you choose for a demonstration in support of e. g. *Black Lives Matter* or an end to police violence against blacks?

Discuss in class.

1 I am happy to join with you today in what will go down in history as the greatest demonstration for freedom in the history of our nation.

2 Five score[1] years ago a great American, in whose symbolic shadow we stand today, signed the Emancipation Proclamation[2]. This momentous[3] decree[4] came as a great beacon[5] light of hope to millions of Negro slaves who had been seared[6] in the flames of withering[7] injustice. It came as a joyous daybreak to end the long night of captivity.

But 100 years later the Negro still is not free. One hundred years later, the life of the Negro is still badly crippled by the manacles[8] of segregation and the chains of discrimination. One hundred years later, the Negro lives on a lonely island of poverty in the midst of a vast ocean of material prosperity. One hundred years later, the Negro is still languished[9] in the corners of American society and finds himself in exile in his own land. And so we've come here today to dramatize a shameful situation.

3 In a sense we've come to our nation's capital to cash a check. When the architects of our Republic wrote the magnificent[10] words of the Constitution and the Declaration of Independence, they were signing a promissory note[11] to which every American was to fall heir[12]. This note was a promise that all men – yes, black men as well as white men – would be guaranteed the "unalienable rights" of "Life, Liberty and the pursuit of Happiness." It is obvious today that America has defaulted[13] on this promissory note insofar as her citizens of color are concerned. Instead of honoring this sacred obligation[14], America has given the Negro people a bad check, a check which has come back marked 'insufficient funds[15].' But we refuse to believe that the bank of justice is bankrupt. We refuse to believe that there are insufficient funds in the great vaults[16] of opportunity of this nation.

[1] **score** twenty – [2] **Emancipation Proclamation** (1963) proclamation by Abraham Lincoln that changed the legal status of the slaves to free men – [3] **momentous** *folgenschwer* – [4] **decree** *Erlass* – [5] **beacon** *Leuchtfeuer* – [6] **to sear** to burn the surface of sth. with sudden very strong heat – [7] **to wither** to become weak and dry and decay; *verwelken, verkümmern* – [8] **manacles** *Handfesseln* – [9] **to languish** to exist in an unpleasant and unwanted situation – [10] **magnificent** very good and beautiful – [11] **promissory note** *Schuldbrief, Wechsel* – [12] **to fall heir** (*idm.*) to inherit sth.; *etw. erben* – [13] **to default** to fail to do sth. – [14] **obligation** *Verpflichtung* – [15] **insufficient funds** a situation when an account does not have enough money in it to pay a cheque that has been written – [16] **vault** here: *Schatzkammer*

And so we've come to cash this check, a check that will give us upon demand the riches of freedom and the security of justice.

4 We have also come to this hallowed[17] spot to remind America of the fierce[18] urgency[19] of Now. This is no time to engage in the luxury of cooling off or to take the tranquilizing[20] drug of gradualism[21]. Now is the time to make real the promises of democracy. Now is the time to rise from the dark and desolate[22] valley of segregation to the sunlit path of racial justice. Now is the time to lift our nation from the quicksands[23] of racial injustice to the solid rock of brotherhood. Now is the time to make justice a reality for all of God's children. [...]

5 [...] We must forever conduct[24] our struggle on the high plane of dignity and discipline. We must not allow our creative protests to degenerate into physical violence. Again and again we must rise to the majestic heights of meeting physical force with soul force.
The marvelous new militancy which has engulfed[25] the Negro community must not lead us to a distrust of all white people, for many of our white brothers, as evidenced by their presence here today, have come to realize that their destiny is tied up with our destiny. And they have come to realize that their freedom is inextricably[26] bound to our freedom.
We cannot walk alone.
And as we walk, we must make the pledge[27] that we shall always march ahead.
We cannot turn back.

There are those who are asking the devotees[28] of civil rights, "When will you be satisfied?" We can never be satisfied as long as the Negro is the victim of the unspeakable horrors of police brutality. [...]

6 And so, even though we face the difficulties of today and tomorrow, I still have a dream. It is a dream deeply rooted in the American dream.
I have a dream that one day this nation will rise up and live out the true meaning of its creed[29]: "We hold these truths to be self-evident, that all men are created equal."
I have a dream that one day on the red hills of Georgia, the sons of former slaves and the sons of former slave owners will be able to sit together at the table of brotherhood.
I have a dream that one day even the state of Mississippi, a state sweltering[29] with the heat of injustice, sweltering with the heat of oppression, will be transformed into an oasis of freedom and justice.
I have a dream that my four little children will one day live in a nation where they will not be judged by the color of their skin but by the content of their character.
I have a dream today.
I have a dream that one day, down in Alabama, with its vicious[30] racists, with its governor having his lips dripping with the words of interposition[31] and nullification[32], one day right there in Alabama little black boys and black girls will be able to join hands with little white boys and white girls as sisters and brothers. [...]

Martin Luther King, Jr., 1963, at the March on Washington; https://www.achives.gov/files/press/exhibits/dream-speech.pdf [06.06.2020]

COMPREHENSION

1. In a first reading, get an overview of the overall atmosphere and the relevant topics referred to by Martin Luther King.

Tip: You can also listen to the full speech to get a better impression of Martin Luther King's abilities as a speaker: https://www.americanrhetoric.com/speeches/mlkihaveadream.htm.

2. Now team up in groups of 3–4 students and, after reading the extracts from the speech a second time, compile a mind map (see example on p. 32) that visualizes the aspects contained in the speech.

[17] **hallowed** very respected and praised because of great importance – [18] **fierce** strong, powerful and frightening – [19] **urgency** *Dringlichkeit* – [20] **tranquilizing** *betäubend, ruhigstellend* – [21] **gradualism** here: *Politik der kleinen Schritte* – [22] **desolate** empty and unattractive – [23] **quicksand** *Treibsand* – [24] **conduct** organize and perform a particular activity – [25] **to engulf** to surround and cover sb./sth. completely – [26] **inextricably** unable to be separated or escaped from – [27] **to pledge** to make serious or formal promise to do sth. – [28] **devotee** a person who strongly admires sb./sth.; *Verehrer* – [29] **creed** (*fml.*) a set of beliefs that influences the way you live; *Überzeugung, Glaubensbekenntnis* – [30] **to swelter** to feel very hot – [31] **vicious** *teuflisch* – [32] **interposition** the right of states to protect their interests from federal violation; *Einmischung* – [33] **nullification** theory that states can oppose federal law they consider unconstitutional; here: the law prohibiting racial segregation; *Nichtigerklärung*

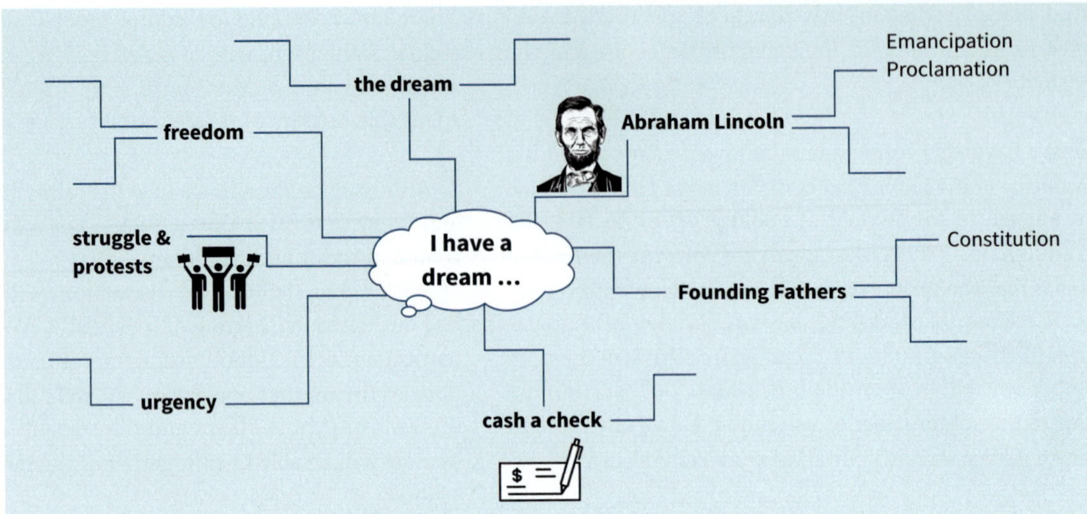

3. Write a summary of the speech of about 200 – 250 words, leaving out irrelevant details and Martin Luther King's embellishments (*Ausschmückungen*) and using the simple present as the predominant tense.

ANALYSIS

4. Martin Luther King uses various rhetorical and stylistic devices to illustrate and emphasize his message. Together with a partner, analyse and explain their meaning and function. Focus on these devices:
   - alliteration and anaphora
   - repetition and parallelism
   - metaphors and personifications
   - antithesis (contrast)
   - references to politics and history

5. Divide the class into groups, with each group working with one of the cartoons.

   Step 1: Describe the cartoons in detail, using the help given in the Tips on vocab boxes.

   Step 2: Explain the criticism and message expressed by the cartoonist, paying attention to visual and textual elements.

   Step 3: Now, the groups mix and describe and explain the cartoons to each other.

1

2

Tips on vocab

billboard ■ banner headline ■ capital letters in bold print ■ portrait of Martin Luther King Jr. ■ ladder ■ cans of white paint ■ to paint over

Tips on vocab

to walk in a crowd (of people) ■ to hold up placards ■ to demonstrate for/against sth. ■ a long line of protesters

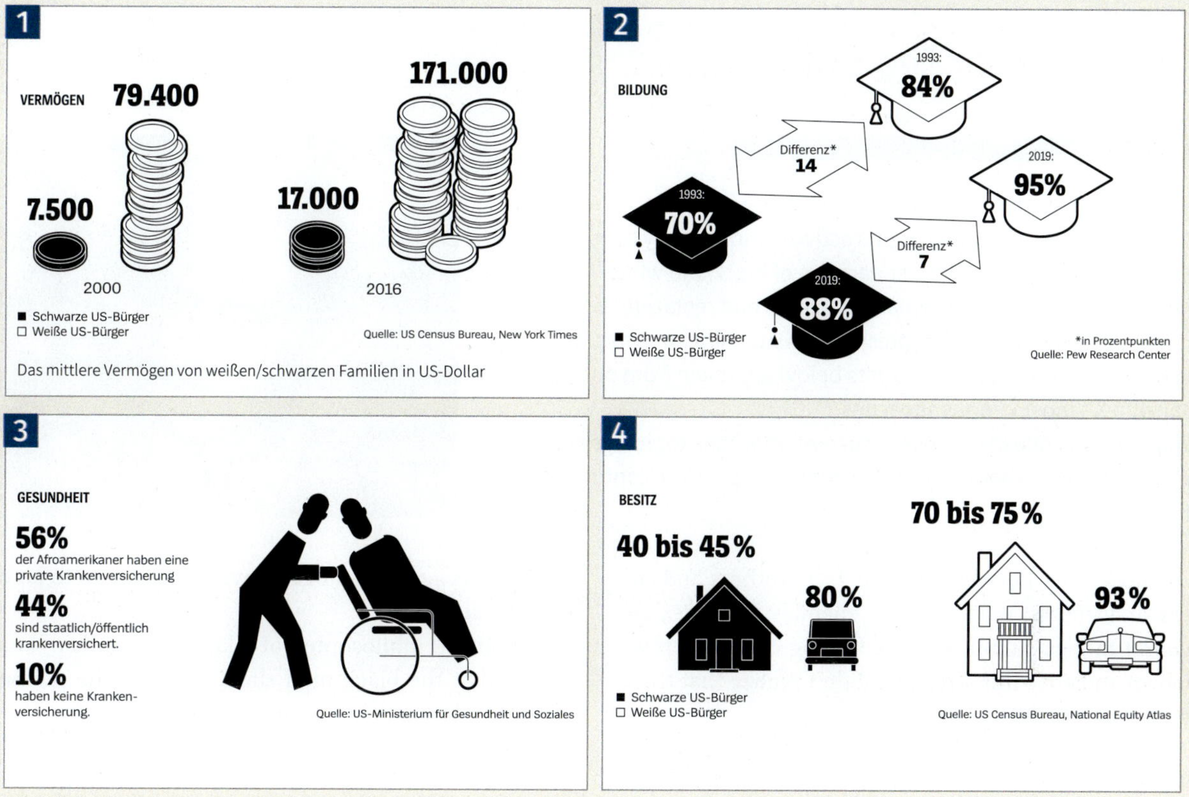

https://www.spiegel.de/politik/ausland/usa-nach-dem-fall-george-floyd-erschiesst-mich-nicht-a-00000000-0002-0001-0000-000171527072, 12.06.2020 [14.06.2020]

6. Six decades after Martin Luther King's famous speech, social justice, equality and "cashing a check" are still far from being reality for many African Americans.
Examine the infographics above and explain the differences between white and African Americans in the U. S. today.

ACTIVITIES

7. You are a young civil rights activist who supports the *Black Lives Matter* initiative. In response to Martin Luther King's famous speech and looking at its demands and messages today, write an article for an internet blog, in which you assess whether (or which of) Martin Luther King's ideas are still relevant today.

8. Some of the more radical African American civil rights activists and leaders disapprovingly called Martin Luther King a "white negro/nigger" because they thought he was too friendly and lenient with America's white population. Against the background that there is still so much racism and injustice today – do you think that this judgement is (partly) true and that African Americans should have been more radical? Discuss in class.

Malcolm X

The Ballot[1] or the Bullet[2]

AWARENESS

Malcolm X (1925 – 1965), born Malcolm Little, was an African American Muslim minister and human rights activist who strongly advocated black empowerment and the separation of black and white. In his autobiography, Malcom X explained that he had replaced his "slave name" Little by "X", which represents his true African name, one he would never know. The extracts below are taken from one of Malcolm X's most famous speeches.
What does the title of the speech suggest about the topics Malcolm X is going to speak about? Speculate about the possible content of the speech.

Mr. Moderator, Reverend Cleage, [...] brothers and sisters, and friends, and I see some enemies. [*laughter, applause*] In fact, I think we'd be fooling ourselves if we had an audience this large and didn't realize that there were some enemies present.

This afternoon we want to talk about the ballot or the bullet. The ballot or the bullet explains itself. But before we get into it, since this is the year of the ballot or the bullet, I would like to clarify some things that refer to me personally, concerning my own personal position. [...]

I'm a Black Nationalist freedom fighter. [*applause*] Islam is my religion but I believe my religion is my personal business. [*applause*] It governs my personal life, my personal morals. And my religious philosophy is personal between me and the God in whom I believe, just as the religious philosophy of these others is between them and the God in whom they believe. And this is best this way. Were we to come out here discussing religion, we'd have too many differences from the outstart and we could never get together.

So today, though Islam is my religious philosophy, my political, economic, and social philosophy is black nationalism. You and I – [*applause*] As I say, if we bring up religion, we'll have differences, we'll have arguments, and we'll never be able to get together. But if we keep our religion at home, keep our religion in the closet[3], keep our religion between ourselves and our God, but when we come out here, we have a fight that's common to all[4] of us against an enemy who is common to all of us. [*applause*]

The political philosophy of black nationalism only means that the black man should control the politics and the politicians in his own community. [...]

The economic philosophy of black nationalism only means that we should own and operate and control the economy of our community. You would never have found – you can't open up a black store in a white community. White men won't even patronize[5] you. And he's not wrong. He's got sense enough to look out for himself. It's you who don't have sense enough to look out for yourself. [*applause*]

The white man, the white man is too intelligent to let someone else come and gain control of the economy of his community. But you will let anybody come in and control the economy of your community, control the housing, control the education, control the jobs, control the businesses, under the pretext[6] that you want to integrate. Nah, you're out of your mind. [*applause*]

The political ... the economic philosophy of black nationalism only means that we have to become involved in a program of reeducation, to educate our people into the importance of knowing that when you spend your dollar out of the community in which you live, the community in which you spend your money becomes richer and richer, the community out of which you take your money becomes poorer and poorer. And because these Negroes, who have been misled, misguided, are

[1] **ballot** an occasion when people vote on sth.; *Wahlgang* – [2] **bullet** a small metal object that is shot from a gun – [3] **in the closet** private – [4] **common to all** shared by all – [5] **to patronize** to speak or behave towards sb. as if they were stupid or not important – [6] **pretext** *Vorwand*

breaking their necks[7] to take their money and spend it with the Man, the Man is becoming richer and richer, and you're becoming poorer and poorer. And then what happens? The community in which you live becomes a slum. It becomes a ghetto. The conditions become rundown. And then you have the audacity[8] to complain about poor housing in a rundown community, while you're running down yourselves when you take your dollar out. [*applause*] [...]

Whether you are a Christian or a Muslim or a nationalist, we all have the same problem. They don't hang you because you're a Baptist; they hang you 'cause you're black. [*applause*] They don't attack me because I'm a Muslim. They attack me 'cause I'm black. They attacked all of us for the same reason. All of us catch hell[9] from the same enemy. We're all in the same bag, in the same boat.

We suffer political oppression, economic exploitation and social degradation[10]. All of 'em from the same enemy. The government has failed us. You can't deny that. Any time you're living in the 20th century, 1964, and you walking around here singing "We Shall Overcome," the government has failed you. [*applause*] This is part of what's wrong with you, you do too much singing. [*laughter*] Today it's time to stop singing and start swinging[11]. [*laughter, applause*] [...]

We need a self-help program, a do-it-yourself philosophy, a do-it-right-now philosophy, an it's-already-too-late philosophy. This is what you and I need to get on with. And the only time – the only way we're going to solve our problem is with a self-help program. Before we can get a self-help program started, we have to have a self-help philosophy. Black nationalism is a self-help philosophy. [...]

Every nation in Asia gained its independence through the philosophy of nationalism. Every nation on the African continent that has gotten its independence brought it about through the philosophy of nationalism. And it will take black nationalism to bring about the freedom of 22 million Afro-Americans, here in this country, where we have suffered colonialism for the past 400 years. [*applause*]

America is just as much a colonial power as England ever was. America is just as much a colonial power as France ever was. In fact, America is more so a colonial power than they, because she is a hypocritical[12] colonial power behind it. [*applause*] What is 20th century – what, what do you call second-class citizenship? Why, that's colonization. Second-class citizenship is nothing but 20th century slavery. How you gonna tell me you're a second-class citizen? They don't have second-class citizenship in any other government on this Earth. They just have slaves and people who are free! Well, this country is a hypocrite[13]! They try and make you think they set you free by calling you a second-class citizen. No, you're nothing but a 20th century slave. [*applause*]

Just as it took nationalism to remove colonialism from Asia and Africa, it'll take black nationalism today to remove colonialism from the backs and the minds of twenty-two million Afro-Americans here in this country. And 1964 looks like it might be the year of the ballot or the bullet. [*applause*]

[...] And in 1964, this seems to be the year. Because what can the white man use, now, to fool us? After he put down that March on Washington – and you see all through that now, he tricked you, had you marching down to Washington. Had you marching back and forth between the feet of a dead man named Lincoln and another dead man named George Washington, singing, "We Shall Overcome." [*applause*]

He made a chump[14] out of you. He made a fool out of you. He made you think you were going somewhere and you end up going nowhere but between Lincoln and Washington. [*laughter*]

So today our people are disillusioned. They've become disenchanted[15]. They've become dissatisfied. And in their frustrations they want action. And in 1964 you'll see this young black man, this new generation, asking for the ballot or the bullet. That old Uncle Tom action[16] is outdated. The young generation don't want to hear anything about "the odds[17] are against us." What do we care about odds? [*applause*]

When this country here was first being founded, there were thirteen colonies. The whites were colonized. They were fed up with this taxation without representation[18]. So some of them stood up and said, "Liberty or death!" I went to a white school over here in Mason,

[7] **to break one's neck to do sth.** *sich überanstrengen um etw. zu tun* – [8] **audacity** daring rudeness, lack of respect – [9] **to catch hell** (*coll.*) *Schimpfe bekommen* – [10] **degradation** the loss of self-respect; *Erniedrigung* – [11] **to swing** here: (*infml.*) to arrange for sth. to happen, often by slightly dishonest means; also: to play lively music – [12] **hypocritical** [ˌhɪpəˈkrɪt̬ɪkəl] *scheinheilig* – [13] **hypocrite** [ˈhɪpəˌkrɪt] *Heuchler* – [14] **chump** (*old use, infml.*) a silly or stupid person – [15] **disenchanted** *ernüchtert* – [16] **Uncle Tom action** a black man considered to be overly obedient and servile to white people – [17] **the odds** *Gewinnchancen* – [18] **(no) taxation without representation** political slogan of the 1700s, expressing the colonists' anger about being taxed but having no political voice in parliament

Michigan. The white man made the mistake of letting me read his history books. [*laughter*] He made the mistake of teaching me that Patrick Henry[19] was a patriot, and George Washington[20] – wasn't nothing non-violent about ol' Pat, or George Washington. "Liberty or death" was what brought about the freedom of whites in this country from the English. [*applause*]
They didn't care about the odds. Why, they faced the wrath[21] of the entire British Empire. And in those days, they used to say that the British Empire was so vast and so powerful that the sun would never set on it. This is how big it was, yet these thirteen little scrawny[22] states, tired of taxation without representation, tired of being exploited and oppressed and degraded, told that big British Empire, "Liberty or death." [...]
I'm one of the 22 million black victims of the Democrats. One of the 22 million black victims of the Republicans and one of the 22 million black victims of Americanism. [*applause*] And when I speak, I don't speak as a Democrat or a Republican, nor an American. I speak as a victim of America's so-called democracy. You and I have never seen democracy – all we've seen is hypocrisy. [*applause*]
When we open our eyes today and look around America, we see America not through the eyes of someone who has enjoyed the fruits of Americanism. We see America through the eyes of someone who has been the victim of Americanism. We don't see any American dream. We've experienced only the American nightmare. We haven't benefited from America's democracy. We've only suffered from America's hypocrisy. And the generation that's coming up now can see it. And are not afraid to say it. If you go to jail, so what? If you're black, you were born in jail. [*applause*] [...]
This is why I say it's the ballot or the bullet. It's liberty or it's death. It's freedom for everybody or freedom for nobody. [*applause*] America today finds herself in a unique situation. Historically, revolutions are bloody, oh yes they are. They have never had a bloodless revolution. Or a non-violent revolution. That don't happen even in Hollywood. [*laughter*] You don't have a revolution in which you love your enemy. And you don't have a revolution in which you are begging the system of exploitation to integrate you into it. Revolutions overturn[23] systems. Revolutions destroy systems. [...]
I hope that the white man can see this. 'Cause if you don't see it you're finished. If you don't see it you're going to become involved in some action in which you don't have a chance. We don't care anything about your atomic bomb; it's useless, because other countries have atomic bombs. When two or three different countries have atomic bombs, nobody can use them. So it means that the white man today is without a weapon. If you want some action you've got to come on down to Earth, and there's more black people on Earth than there are white people. [*applause*] [...]
So I say in my conclusion, the only way we're going to solve it: we got to unite. We got to work together in unity and harmony. And black nationalism is the key. How we gonna overcome the tendency to be at each other's throats that always exists in our neighborhood? And the reason this tendency exists – the strategy of the white man has always been divide and conquer[24]. He keeps us divided in order to conquer us. He tells you, I'm for separation and you for integration, and keep us fighting with each other. No, I'm not for separation and you're not for integration, what you and I are for is freedom. [*applause*] Only, you think that integration will get you freedom; I think that separation will get me freedom. We both got the same objective[25], we just got different ways of getting' at it. [*applause*] [...]

Malcolm X, 12 April 1964, King Solomon Baptist Church, Detroit, Michigan; https://americanradioworks.publicradio.org/features/blackspeech/mx.html; [07.08.2020]

COMPREHENSION

1. Point out how Malcolm X defines his personal and political background.

2. Describe Malcolm X's ideas concerning the "economic philosophy of black nationalism".

[19] **Patrick Henry** (1736 – 1799) American planter, slaveholder and politician; one of the Founding Fathers of the USA – [20] **George Washington** (1732 – 1799) first president of the USA, one of the Founding Fathers – [21] **wrath** extreme anger – [22] **scrawny** (*infml. derog.*) very thin because you don't get enough to eat – [23] **overturn** to bring to an end suddenly; *stürzen* – [24] **divide and conquer** (from the Latin 'divide et impera') to make a group of people disagree and fight with one another so that they won't join forces; strategy of the American colonists to defeat the British army – [25] **objective** aim

3. Present Malcolm X's philosophy of (black) nationalism as a "self-help program" to overcome colonization and colonialism.

4. What does Malcolm X criticize about the March on Washington?

ANALYSIS

5. Explain Malcolm X's juxtaposition of the first thirteen colonies' fight against the British Empire and the black people's fight against Americanism. Copy the grid and collect information from the speech.

the first 13 colonies/American Revolution	black nationalism
• no taxation without representation • Liberty or death! • …	• 20th century slavery • American nightmare • …

6. In conclusion, Malcolm X reflects on integration versus separation. Explain his line of argument. Examine Malcolm X's use of rhetorical devices and focus on these aspects:
   - the use of personal pronouns
   - the use of contrast/antithesis
   - historical references
   - irony
   - repetition

   Tip: You can also listen to the speech on:
   https://americanradioworks.publicradio.org/features/blackspeech/mx.html

7. If you have dealt with Martin Luther King's speech *I Have a Dream* (pp. 30 ff.), compare it to Malcolm X's speech.
   - How do the basic political and societal ideas of these two civil rights activists differ?
   - How do the speeches differ in their use of language and overall tone?

ACTIVITIES

8. Malcolm X states that "America is as much a colonial power as England ever was" and that blacks are nothing but 20th century slaves.
   Do you think that this is also true for the 21st century? Discuss your views in class.

9. Do a project on Malcolm X and his far more radical political ideas than Martin Luther King's.
   You may want to use these weblinks for your research:
   - https://www.britannica.com/biography/Malcolm-X
   - https://www.bpb.de/politik/hintergrund-aktuell/201549/1965-ermordung-von-malcolm-x
   - https://www.ushistory.org/us/54h.asp

Lyndon B. Johnson

We Shall Overcome[1]

AWARENESS

In the wake of[2] the Civil War (1861–1865), the Southern states of the U. S. established a set of rules and laws aimed at "restoring all of slavery but its name" and establishing a policy called "equal but separate".
Find information on how African Americans were systematically disadvantaged and politically and socially marginalized. Do research on:

- https://en.wikipedia.org/wiki/Jim_Crow_laws
- https://en.wikipedia.org/wiki/Literacy_test
- https://allthatsinteresting.com/voting-literacy-test
- https://www.crmvet.org/info/lithome.htm
- https://en.wikipedia.org/wiki/Selma_to_Montgomery_marches

President Johnson signing the Civil Rights Bill; behind him: Martin Luther King Jr.

1 Mr. Speaker, Mr. President, Members of the Congress. – I speak tonight for the dignity of man and the destiny of democracy.

I urge every member of both parties, Americans of all religions and of all colors, from every section of this country, to join me in that cause.

At times, history and fate meet at a single time in a single place to shape a turning point in man's unending search for freedom. So it was at Lexington and Concord[3]. So it was a century ago at Appomattox[4]. So it was last week in Selma[5], Alabama.

There, long-suffering men and women peacefully protested the denial of their rights as Americans. Many were brutally assaulted. One good man, a man of God, was killed.

There is no cause for pride in what has happened in Selma. There is no cause for self-satisfaction in the long denial of equal rights of millions of Americans. But there is cause for hope and for faith in our democracy in what is happening here tonight.

For the cries of pain and the hymns and protests of oppressed people have summoned[6] into convocation[7] all the majesty of this great government – the government of the greatest nation on earth.

2 Our mission is at once the oldest and the most basic of this country: to right wrong, to do justice, to serve man.

In our time we have come to live with moments of great crisis. Our lives have been marked with debate about great issues; issues of war and peace, issues of prosperity and depression. But rarely in any time does an issue lay bare[8] the secret heart of America itself. [...]

There is no Negro problem. There is no Southern problem. There is no Northern problem. There is only an American problem. And we are met here tonight as Americans – not as Democrats or Republicans – we are met here as Americans to solve that problem.

3 This was the first nation in the history of the world to be founded with a purpose. The great phrases of that purpose still sound in every American heart, North and South: "All men are created equal" – "government by consent of the governed" – "give me liberty or give me death[9]." Well, those are not just clever words, and those are not just empty theories. In their name Americans have fought and died for two centuries, and tonight around the world they stand there as guardians[10] of our liberty, risking their lives.

[1] **We shall overcome** a gospel song which became a protest song and symbol of the civil rights movement – [2] **in the wake of** happening after or because of sth. – [3] **(battles of) Lexington and Concord** the first battles of the American Revolutionary War, fought in April 1775 – [4] **Appomattox** place in Virginia where one of the last battles of the Civil War (1861–1865) was fought – [5] **Selma** town in Alabama where state troopers attacked civil rights demonstrators on "Bloody Sunday", 7 March 1965 – [6] **to summon** to order sb. to come – [7] **convocation** (*fml.*) a large formal meeting – [8] **to lay bare** *bloßlegen* – [9] **give me liberty or give me death** a quotation by Patrick Henry, one of the Founding Fathers of the U. S., in 1775 – [10] **guardian** (*fml.*) sb. who protects

Those words are a promise to every citizen that he shall share in the dignity of man. This dignity cannot be found in a man's possessions; it cannot be found in his power, or in his position. It really rests on his right to be treated as a man equal in opportunity to all others. It says that he shall share in freedom, he shall choose his leaders, educate his children, and provide for his family according to his ability and his merits[11] as a human being.

To apply any other test – to deny a man his hopes because of his color or race, his religion or the place of his birth – is not only to do injustice, it is to deny America and to dishonor the dead who gave their lives for American freedom.

Our fathers believed that if this noble view of the rights of man was to flourish[12], it must be rooted in democracy. The most basic right of all was the right to choose your own leaders. The history of this country, in large measure[13], is the history of the expansion of that right to all of our people.

4 Many of the issues of civil rights are very complex and most difficult. But about this there can and should be no argument. Every American citizen must have an equal right to vote. There is no reason which can excuse the denial of that right. There is no duty which weighs more heavily on us than the duty we have to ensure that right.

Yet the harsh Act is that in many places in this country men and women are kept from voting simply because they are Negroes. [...]

In such a case our duty must be clear to all of us. The Constitution says that no person shall be kept from voting because of his race or his color. We have all sworn an oath before God to support and to defend that Constitution. We must now act in obedience[14] to that oath. [...]

5 I have had prepared a more comprehensive[15] analysis of the legislation which I had intended to transmit to the clerk[16] tomorrow but which I will submit[17] to the clerks tonight. But I want to really discuss the main proposals of this legislation.

This bill will strike down[18] restrictions to voting in all elections – federal, state, and local – which have been used to deny Negroes the right to vote.

This bill will establish a simple, uniform standard which cannot be used, however ingenious[19] the effort, to flout[20] our Constitution.

It will provide for citizens to be registered by officials of the United States Government if the state officials refuse to register them.

It will eliminate[21] tedious[22], unnecessary lawsuits[23] which delay the right to vote. Finally, this legislation will ensure that properly registered individuals are not prohibited from voting. [...]

Open your polling places[24] to all your people.

Allow men and women to register and vote whatever the color of their skin.

Extend the rights of citizenship to every citizen of this land.

There is no constitutional issue here. The command of the Constitution is plain[25].

There is no moral issue. It is wrong – deadly wrong – to deny any of your fellow Americans the right to vote in this country.

There is no issue of states' rights or national rights. There is only the struggle for human rights. [...]

6 But even if we pass this bill, the battle will not be over. What happened in Selma is part of a far larger movement which reaches into every section and state of America. It is the effort of American Negroes to secure for themselves the full blessings of American life.

Their cause must be our cause too. Because it is not just Negroes, but really it is all of us, who must overcome the crippling[26] legacy[27] of bigotry[28] and injustice.

And we shall overcome.

As a man whose roots go deeply into Southern soil I know how agonizing[29] racial feelings are. I know how difficult it is to reshape the attitudes and the structure of our society.

But a century has passed, more than a hundred years, since the Negro was freed.

And he is not fully free tonight.

[11] **merit** the quality of being good and deserving praise; *Verdienst* – [12] **to flourish** to be active and successful – [13] **measure** *Maßnahme* – [14] **obedience** the fact that sb. does what he is told to – [15] **comprehensive** complete and including everything that is necessary – [16] **clerk** a person who works in an office – [17] **to submit** *etw. vorlegen, einreichen* – [18] **to strike down sth.** (*phr. v.*) to decide that a law is illegal and should be ignored – [19] **ingenious** very intelligent and skilful – [20] **to flout** *sich über etw. hinwegsetzen* – [21] **to eliminate** to take away sb./sth. – [22] **tedious** long and tiring – [23] **lawsuit** *Gerichtsfall* – [24] **polling place** *Wahllokal* – [25] **plain** obvious and clear to understand – [26] **crippling** causing serious injuries or harm – [27] **legacy** ['legəsi] sth. that is part of your history and that remains from an earlier time; *Vermächtnis* – [28] **bigotry** ['bɪgətri] *Fanatismus* – [29] **agonizing** causing extreme physical or mental pain

It was more than a hundred years ago that Abraham Lincoln, a great President of another party, signed the Emancipation Proclamation[30], but emancipation is a proclamation and not a fact.

A century has passed, more than a hundred years, since equality was promised.

And yet the Negro is not equal.

A century has passed since the day of promise, and the promise is unkept.

The time of justice has now come. I tell you that I believe sincerely that no force can hold it back. It is right in the eyes of man and God that it should come. And when it does, I think that day will brighten the lives of every American. For Negroes are not the only victims. How many white children have gone uneducated, how many white families have lived in stark[31] poverty, how many white lives have been scarred[32] by fear, because we wasted our energy and our substance to maintain the barriers of hatred and terror?

And so I say to all of you here, and to all in the nation tonight, that those who appeal to you to hold on to the past do so at the cost of denying you your future. This great, rich, restless country can offer opportunity and education and hope to all: black and white, North and South, sharecropper[33] and city dweller. These are the enemies: poverty, ignorance, disease. They are our enemies and not our fellow man, not our neighbor. And these enemies too, poverty, disease and ignorance, we shall overcome. [...]

7 The real hero of this struggle is the American Negro. His actions and protests, his courage to risk safety and even to risk his life, have awakened the conscience[34] of this nation. His demonstrations have been designed to call attention to injustice, designed to provoke change, designed to stir reform.

He has called upon us to make good[35] the promise of America. And who among us can say that we would have made the same progress were it not for his persistent[36] bravery, and his faith in American democracy.

For at the real heart of battle for equality is a deep seated belief in the democratic process. Equality depends not on the force of arms or tear gas but upon the force of moral right; not on recourse[37] to violence but on respect for law and order.

There have been many pressures upon your President and there will be others as the days come and go. But I pledge[38] to you tonight that we intend to fight this battle where it should be fought – in the courts, and in the Congress, and in the hearts of men.

We must preserve the right of free speech and the right of free assembly. But the right of free speech does not carry with it, as has been said, the right to holler fire[39] in a crowded theater. We must preserve the right to free assembly, but free assembly does not carry with it the right to block public thoroughfares[40] to traffic. [...]

8 The bill I am presenting to you will be known as a civil rights bill. But, in a larger sense, most of the program I am recommending is a civil rights program. Its object is to open the city of hope to all people of all races. Because all Americans just must have the right to vote. And we are going to give them that right.

All Americans must have the privileges of citizenship regardless of race. And they are going to have those privileges of citizenship regardless of race. [...]

This is the richest and most powerful country which ever occupied the globe. The might of past empires is little compared to ours. But I do not want to be the President who built empires, or sought[41] grandeur[42], or extended[43] dominion[44].

I want to be the President who educated young children to the wonders of their world. I want to be the President who helped to feed the hungry and to prepare them to be taxpayers instead of tax eaters.

I want to be the President who helped the poor to find their own way and who protected the right of every citizen to vote in every election.

I want to be the President who helped to end hatred among his fellow men and who promoted love among the people of all races, all regions and all parties.

I want to be the President who helped to end war among the brothers of this earth. [...]

Lyndon B. Johnson, 15 March 1965; https://usa.usembassy.de/etexts/speeches/rhetoric/lbjoerco.htm [07.08.2020]

[30] **Emancipation Proclamation** on 1 January 1863, President Abraham Lincoln proclaimed the freedom of all slaves – [31] **stark** extreme – [32] **scarred** *gezeichnet* – [33] **sharecropper** *Landpächter*– [34] **conscience** *Gewissen* – [35] **to make good** to put into effect; *einlösen* – [36] **persistent** lasting for a long time and difficult to get rid of – [37] **recourse to** (*fml.*) help of –[38] **to pledge** to make a serious formal promise – [39] **to holler fire** (*infml.*) to cause a panic by shouting fire – [40] **thoroughfare** a main road for public use – [41] **to seek (sought, sought)** (*fml.*) to try to find or get sth. – [42] **grandeur** the quality of being very large, important and special and attracting admiration – [43] **to extend** to make sth. bigger; to add sth. – [43] **dominion** control over a country or people

COMPREHENSION

The Civil Rights Act of 1964 is one of the most important bills to prohibit
a) the unequal application of voter registration requirements (e. g. literacy tests),
b) racial segregation in schools, employment and public accommodations.
The bill had already been proposed by John F. Kennedy in 1963, and was pushed forward by Lyndon B. Johnson after Kennedy's assassination. In his speech to Congress, Johnson urges the delegates to support his fight for equality and democracy.

1. Read parts 1 – 4 of the speech and complete the sentences below, using information from the text.
   a) Lyndon B. Johnson's reason for delivering this speech is ...
   b) President Johnson's examples of turning points in history refer to ...
   c) Americans can rely on American democracy because ...
   d) The U. S. government's mission is ...
   e) The Founding Fathers' purpose in founding the U.S. was ...
   f) The dignity of man is based on ...
   g) Denying people the right to register and vote means ...
   h) The most basic democratic right is ...
   i) Many men and women are still not allowed to vote because ...
   j) Politicians have sworn ...

2. Read part 5 and outline the benefits of the new bill.

3. Present what part 6 reveals about
   a) the efforts white and African Americans have to make,
   b) the problems whites and African Americans have to face.

4. Describe what democratic and moral rights were claimed by the actions and protests of African Americans (cf. part 7).

5. Outline the "privileges of citizenship" which President Johnson promises in part 8 of the speech.

ANALYSIS

6. In order to convince the members of Congress of his ideas, Lyndon B. Johnson has employed many stylistic and rhetorical devices to emphasize the message and appeal of his speech.
Find examples in the text and explain how they support Johnson's intention. Focus on the following rhetorical devices:
- repetition – parallelism – enumeration
- alliteration – anaphora
- positive and negative emotive words
- metaphorical expressions
- patterns of solidarity and identification (e. g. pronouns)
- climax

7. a) Examine the concluding paragraph of Johnson's speech and explain what kind of president he wants to be.
   b) Compare his definition of the presidency to what is explained about a president's duties and obligations in the Constitution (cf. pp. 23 f.). Which parallels and differences can you detect?

ACTIVITIES

8. In the title and in the course of his speech, Johnson refers to the title of an old gospel song, *We shall overcome*, which has become the unofficial anthem of the civil rights movement.
@ Do further research on the song on the internet and find out about its meaning and relevance today.

9. The Civil Rights Act of 1964 was adopted in the midst of the unrest, fighting and struggles of the civil rights movement.
What do you imagine people's reactions to it were back then? Do you think that African Americans were enthusiastic or more critical about these political efforts? Discuss in class.

GRAMMAR / LANGUAGE

10. Reread parts 5 and 8 and report them to a friend who hasn't read Johnson's speech. Use **indirect speech** and make sure to use the correct **tenses** and to **backshift** if necessary. Remember to employ suitable **introductory verbs** and phrases.

Example:
Johnson pointed out that he had prepared a more comprehensive analysis of … which he had intended to … the following day … but which he would submit to … .

John Irving

"She was just like our whole country …"

AWARENESS

a) What do you know about the American Hollywood icon Marilyn Monroe?
b) Take a look at the photographs, taken in February 1954 and May 1962, and describe her looks and body language. What impression do you have of her?

1

U.S. President Kennedy (right), his brother, Robert Kennedy (left) with Marilyn Monroe celebrating the President's 45th birthday in May 1962

2

Marilyn Monroe performing in front of over 10,000 GIs on a military base in Korea in February 1954

"Did you hear about Marilyn Monroe?" he asked us again. Suddenly, it didn't sound like a joke. Maybe it's about the Kennedys! I thought.

"No. What about her?" I said.

"She's dead." ... [...]

"An overdose," he said; he sounded disappointed – as if he'd been hoping for something bloodier. "Maybe it was an accident – maybe it was suicide," he said.

Maybe it was the Kennedys. I thought. It made me feel afraid; at first, that summer, it was something vague[1] that had made me feel afraid. Now something concrete made me feel afraid – but my fear itself was still vague: what could Marilyn Monroe's death ever have to do with me?

"IT HAS TO DO WITH ALL OF US," said Owen Meany, when I called him that night. "SHE WAS JUST LIKE OUR WHOLE COUNTRY – NOT QUITE YOUNG ANYMORE, BUT NOT OLD EITHER; A LITTLE BREATHLESS, VERY BEAUTIFUL, MAYBE A LITTLE STUPID, MAYBE A LOT SMARTER THAN SHE SEEMED, AND SHE WAS LOOKING FOR SOMETHING – I THINK SHE WANTED TO BE GOOD. LOOK AT THE MEN IN HER LIFE – JOE DIMAGGIO[2], ARTHUR MILLER[3], MAYBE THE KENNEDYS. LOOK AT HOW GOOD THEY SEEM! LOOK AT HOW DESIRABLE SHE WAS! THAT'S WHAT SHE WAS: SHE WAS DESIRABLE. SHE WAS FUNNY AND SEXY – AND SHE WAS VULNERABLE[4], TOO. SHE WAS NEVER QUITE HAPPY, SHE WAS ALWAYS A LITTLE OVERWEIGHT. SHE WAS JUST LIKE OUR WHOLE COUNTRY, he repeated; he was on a roll[5]. I could hear Hester playing her guitar in the background, as if she were trying to improvise a folk song from everything he said. "AND THOSE MEN," he said. "THOSE FAMOUS, POWERFUL MEN – DID THEY REALLY LOVE HER? DID THEY TAKE CARE OF HER? IF SHE WAS EVER WITH THE KENNEDYS, THEY COULDN'T HAVE LOVED HER – THEY WERE JUST USING HER, THEY WERE JUST BEING CARELESS AND TREATING THEMSELVES TO A THRILL[6]. THAT'S WHAT POWERFUL MEN DO TO THIS COUNTRY – IT'S A BEAUTIFUL, SEXY, BREATHLESS COUNTRY, AND POWERFUL MEN USE IT TO TREAT THEMSELVES TO A THRILL! THEY SAY THEY LOVE IT BUT THEY DON'T MEAN IT. THEY SAY THINGS TO MAKE THEMSELVES APPEAR GOOD – THEY MAKE THEMSELVES APPEAR GOOD – THEY MAKE THEMSELVES APPEAR MORAL. THAT'S WHAT I THOUGHT KENNEDY WAS: A MORALIST. BUT HE WAS JUST GIVING US A SNOW JOB[7], HE WAS JUST BEING A GOOD SEDUCER[8]. I THOUGHT HE WAS A SAVIOR[9]. I THOUGHT HE WANTED TO USE HIS POWER TO DO GOOD. BUT PEOPLE WILL SAY AND DO ANYTHING JUST TO GET POWER; THEN THEY'LL USE THE POWER JUST TO GET A THRILL. MARYLIN MONROE WAS ALWAYS LOOKING FOR THE BEST MAN – MAYBE SHE WANTED THE MAN WITH THE BEST INTEGRITY[10], MAYBE SHE WANTED THE MAN WITH THE MOST ABILITY TO DO GOOD, AND SHE WAS SEDUCED, OVER AND OVER AGAIN – SHE GOT FOOLED, SHE WAS TRICKED, SHE GOT USED, SHE WAS USED UP[11]. JUST LIKE THE COUNTRY. THE COUNTRY WANTS A SAVIOR. THE COUNTRY IS A SUCKER[12] FOR POWERFUL MEN WHO LOOK GOOD. WE THINK THEY'RE MORALISTS AND THEN THEY JUST USE US. THAT'S WHAT'S GOING TO HAPPEN TO YOU AND ME," said Owen Meany. "WE'RE GOING TO BE USED."

from *A Prayer for Owen Meany* by John Irving. Bloomsbury Publishing, London 1989, pp. 446 – 448

COMPREHENSION

The excerpt from the 1989 novel *A Prayer for Owen Meany* by John Irving is a conversation between Owen Meany, the protagonist, and his best friend, John Wheelwright, who is also the narrator. The conversation takes place in August 1962, shortly after the news of Marilyn Monroe's death from an overdose of sleeping pills was announced in the media. She died on 2 August 1962, and her death gave way to much speculation about suicide or murder as well as the involvement of prominent politicians, like the Kennedy brothers, Robert and John F.

[1] **vague** [veɪg] not clearly expressed, known, described – [2] **Joe DiMaggio** (1914 – 1999) one of the greatest U. S. baseball players, married MM in 1954 – [3] **Arthur Miller** (1915 – 2005) U. S. playwright, married MM in 1956 – [4] **vulnerable** easily harmed or hurt – [5] **to be on a roll** (*infml.*) *in Fahrt sein* – [6] **to treat oneself to a thrill** to do sth. exciting that you enjoy e. g. as a reward – [7] **snow job** an effort to deceive with insincere talk – [8] **seducer** sb. who persuades sb. else to have sex with him/her – [9] **savior** a person who rescues sb. from danger or harm – [10] **integrity** honesty – [11] **to use sb./sth. up** to use all of sb./sth. – [12] **sucker for sb./sth.** (*infml.*) person who cannot resist sb./sth. or who likes sb./sth very much and who is easily deceived

1. While reading the excerpt take notes on how Owen Meany describes:

Marilyn Monroe	the country	powerful men/the Kennedys
• not quite young anymore • breathless • …	• not quite young anymore • …	• famous, powerful • …

2. Which (positive) qualities and attributes does Owen Meany link with "the country"?

3. Which attributes does Owen Meany criticize (most) about "the country" and "the powerful men"?

ANALYSIS

4. Explain in what way Marilyn Monroe represents the USA. Which characteristics do they have in common?

5. Analyse and interpret the narrative means and stylistic devices of this fictional text. Pay particular attention to:

- the point of view
- the (contrastive) choice of words
- the use of alliteration and anaphora
- the use of metaphors and similes

Note: The frequent use of capital letters depicts Owen Meany's extraordinary voice: "his vocal cords had not developed fully or else his voice had been injured by the rock dust of his family's business. […] To be heard at all, Owen had to shout through his nose." (pp. 14 ff.)

ACTIVITIES

6. "'It has to do with all of us', said Owen Meany" (ll. 15 f.).
Comment on this statement. Do you agree with Owen Meany?
Discuss and explain to what extent "all of us" are confronted with this kind of abuse of power. (ll. 41 ff.)

7. Can you think of anybody who at present represents (positive or negative) 'typical' American characteristics? Give examples and explain your choice.

Romain Leick, Ralf Neukirch, Jill Lepore

Die Hierarchie der Rassen gehört zur DNA des Landes

AWARENESS

Both of the cartoons below deal with the issue of racism in the U. S. today.

a) Choose one of the cartoons and describe it in detail.

b) Identify what the cartoonists criticize in particular and what message they want to convey.
- Speculate on what makes being 'dark-skinned' so risky 'EVERY.SINGLE.DAY'.
- Why has Uncle Sam lost his 'batteries' and is now an 'empty robot' bowing to the 'white' side?

Discuss your ideas in class.

c) The title of the article states that 'racial hierarchy is part of America's DNA'. Against this background, team up with a partner and tell each other what you anticipate the interview to be about.

1 **SPIEGEL:** Frau Lepore, von außen betrachtet, stellt sich Amerika immer bedrohlicher als eine Nation dar, die aus dem Gleichgewicht geraten[1] ist. Wie lautet die Diagnose[2] der Historikerin?

Lepore: Die auswärtigen Beobachter haben guten Grund, verunsichert zu sein. Es ist sehr schwierig vorherzusagen, was als Nächstes kommt. Historiker können ja keine gerade Zeitlinie ziehen und den Punkt, an dem wir gegenwärtig stehen, exakt bestimmen. Sie sehen sich gern auf einem Berg oder auch nur auf einem Hügel stehen und ins Tal hinunterblicken. Aber wir haben die Talsohle[3] nicht durchschritten, wir sind mittendrin. Amerika ist aus den Fugen[4], die Vereinigten Staaten haben die Orientierung verloren.

SPIEGEL: Ist das eine akute Krise, oder sind die Unruhen, die so viele amerikanische Städte erfasst haben, das Symptom eines chronischen Leidens?

Lepore: Die Tumulte sind zweifellos die Ausgeburt[5] eines unterschwelligen[6] und ungelösten Konflikts in der amerikanischen Geschichte. Proteste, überwiegend friedlich, manchmal auch gewalttätig, dazu die Polizeibrutalität, wie wir sie jetzt erleben, sind ständige Wegbegleiter des amerikanischen Experiments. Rassenunruhen[7] kehren seit dem 19. Jahrhundert immer wieder. Zu Beginn des 20. Jahrhunderts waren mit dem Begriff auf eine fast schon verharmlosende Weise pogromartige[8] Überfälle von Weißen auf Schwarze gemeint. Die Aktivitäten und Lynchmorde des Ku-Klux-Klans sind heute noch berüchtigt.

SPIEGEL: Der Klan existiert noch. Dennoch ist diese Art des rassistischen Terrors, für die er steht, mittlerweile historisch. Wie hat sich die Lage nach dem Aufkommen[9] der Bürgerrechtsbewegung in den Fünfzigern weiterentwickelt?

[1] to be thrown into turmoil – [2] diagnosis – [3] valley bottom – [4] to fall to pieces – [5] spawn – [6] underlying – [7] race riots – [8] pogrom-like – [9] emergence

Lepore: Mindestens bis in die Sechzigerjahre stießen Schwarze, die in großer Zahl vor den Rassengesetzen[10] des Südens in die Städte des Nordens flohen, nach Detroit, Chicago, Milwaukee oder Minneapolis, auf erbitterten[11] Widerstand[12] der ansässigen[13] Weißen, die sie nicht in ihrer Nachbarschaft sehen wollten und in ihnen Konkurrenten um Jobs erblickten. Viele Stadtviertel veränderten sich. Viele soziologische Untersuchungen wurden seitdem gemacht, Berichte geschrieben, Empfehlungen[14] ausgesprochen – meistens wurden sie einfach ignoriert und blieben ohne Folge.

SPIEGEL: Macht man es sich zu einfach, wenn man Rassismus als die Ursünde[15] Amerikas beklagt? Die Sklaverei endete vor 155 Jahren. Wieso konnte das Versprechen von Freiheit, Gleichheit und Gerechtigkeit nicht eingehalten werden?

Lepore: Die Verwirklichung dieser Verheißung ist ein fortwährender Kampf, in den USA genauso wie übrigens im Rest der Welt. Es lässt sich gewiss nicht sagen, es habe keinen Fortschritt gegeben, aber er vollzieht sich furchtbar langsam, unverzeihlich[16] langsam. Die Ursünde ist nicht vergeben, die Erlösung[17] nicht gekommen. Doch die USA sind nicht mehr das gleiche Land wie vor 100 oder 50 Jahren.

SPIEGEL: Rührt nicht dennoch ein großer Teil der schwarzen Verzweiflung aus der unbeantworteten Frage, wie es möglich ist, dass Polizisten noch immer überdurchschnittlich[18] oft schwarze Bürger töten?

Lepore: Und oft genug sogar ungestraft davonkommen. Rassismus tötet, in Amerika ist er nicht nur ein Fehler im System, er ist eine zerstörerische[19] Kraft des Systems.

2 **SPIEGEL:** In den Sechzigerjahren versuchte eine Bewegung um den legendären Pastor Martin Luther King, die schwarzen Amerikaner zu gleichberechtigten Bürgern zu machen. Was unterscheidet heute die Strömung „Black Lives Matter" von der „Black Power"-Bewegung von damals?

Lepore: Ich denke, sie konzentriert sich viel mehr auf die dringend notwendige Reform der Strafverfolgung[20] und des Strafrechts[21]. Die amerikanischen Gefängnisse sind überfüllt mit schwarzen Verurteilten. Die Justizreform ist ein unerledigtes Anliegen der früheren Bürgerrechtsbewegung, die ansonsten wichtige Verbesserungen erreicht hatte. Mit der Wahl von Richard Nixon 1968 zum Präsidenten entstand ein Law-and-Order-Regime, das vielen gegenwärtigen Missständen[22] zugrunde liegt.

SPIEGEL: Die martialische[23] Rhetorik von Donald Trump erinnert in manchem an die apokalyptischen Beschwörungen von Nixon, der nach den Unruhen von 1968 „Städte in Rauch und Flammen" sah. Trump sprach in seiner Amtseinführungsrede[24] vom „Gemetzel[25]" und wütenden Gangs in den Straßen amerikanischer Städte.

Lepore: Wir erleben heute eine Militarisierung der Polizeikräfte, die damals begann, sich unter Ronald Reagan in den Achtzigerjahren fortsetzte und immer noch weitergeht. Dieses Problem hat sich in den vergangenen Jahrzehnten in einer dramatischen Weise verschärft. [...]

SPIEGEL: Donald Trump scheint, wie Nixon, auf die schweigende Mehrheit der konservativen Weißen zu setzen, um seine Macht zu sichern. Sind kaum verbrämte[26] Appelle an Hass, Furcht und weiße Überlegenheitsgefühle[27] noch immer eine Erfolg versprechende Strategie?

Lepore: Tja, es ist schon komisch, dass eine Person, die so einfach gestrickt[28] scheint, so viele Rätsel aufwirft[29]. Vieles von dem, was er von Tag zu Tag tut, scheint nur der Absicherung seiner Macht und seinem politischen Überleben zu dienen. Ob dahinter eine Strategie steckt oder ein impulsgesteuertes[30] Handeln – schwer zu sagen. Kurzfristig mag er den einen oder anderen Erfolg einheimsen, doch ich bezweifle, dass er zu einer langfristigen Planung fähig ist.

SPIEGEL: Für einen Mann, der gemeinhin als inkompetent geschildert wird, hat er in seinem Sinn allerhand erreicht, oder?

Lepore: Vielleicht ist es Wunschdenken[31] meinerseits, auf seine Inkompetenz zu setzen. Es kommt darauf an, was man ihm als Leistungen zuschreibt[32]. Er hat große Teile der Bundesregierung demontiert, er hat die moralische Autorität der USA überall in der Welt beschädigt, er hat die Spaltung der amerikanischen Gesellschaft, die es vor ihm gab, rücksichtslos[33] vertieft und die Gewaltbereitschaft[34] von US-Bürgern gegen andere US-Bürger gefördert. Ich würde diese Taten jedoch nicht als Errungenschaften, sondern als Scheitern[35] ansehen. [...]

[10] racial laws – [11] fierce – [12] resistance – [13] local – [14] recommendation – [15] original sin – [16] unforgivable – [17] redemption – [18] disproportionately – [19] destructive – [20] criminal prosecution – [21] criminal law – [22] grievances – [23] warlike – [24] inaugural address – [25] massacre – [26] hidden – [27] feeling of superiority – [28] simple-minded – [29] to raise questions – [30] impulse-driven – [31] wishful thinking – [32] to attribute sth. to sb. – [33] reckless – [34] readiness to use violence – [35] failure

SPIEGEL: Kann das Schüren[36] von Furcht und Hass am Ende die amerikanische Demokratie bedrohen?
Lepore: Im Anfachen dieser Gefühle ist er zweifellos sehr erfolgreich. Wie weit er diese destruktive Macht entfalten kann, hängt letztlich vom Volk ab. Es sind die Wähler, die dafür die Bedingungen schaffen oder entziehen. Die Geschichte wird am Ende über seine Präsidentschaft ihr Urteil fällen[37], aber die größere Frage ist die, warum er überhaupt die Präsidentschaftswahl gewinnen konnte, wie die Nation an diesen Punkt gelangen konnte. [...]

3 **SPIEGEL:** Gegenwärtig haben die USA es mit einer dreifachen Krise zu tun: dem lebensbedrohlichen Coronavirus, einem schweren ökonomischen Einbruch, der Gewalt in den Städten. Die schwarze Bevölkerung ist unverhältnismäßig[38] stark betroffen. Ist die Ungleichheit das Grundübel der amerikanischen Gesellschaft, die sich ihrem Anspruch nach immer als eine Gesellschaft der Gleichen betrachtet hat?
Lepore: Unsere Geschichte kreist um diese ewige Spannung zwischen einem politischen Ideal von Gleichheit und Volkssouveränität[39] und einer faktischen Ordnung[40], die durch eine Rassenhierarchie[41] geprägt ist. Das gehört zur DNA des Landes. [...]
SPIEGEL: Was wäre also zu tun?
Lepore: Der erste Schritt wäre, sich der Vergangenheit zu stellen. Sie ist Erbe[42], Last und Geschenk zugleich. Die Vereinigten Staaten haben sich einer solchen Vergangenheitsbewältigung nie unterzogen. Sie wollen nicht über Schuld und Wiedergutmachung[43] grübeln. Die Sklaverei wurde 1865 abgeschafft, aber die Chancengleichheit bis heute nicht erreicht. Dafür hätte man die Freigelassenen mit dem nötigen Startkapital ausstatten müssen, und dafür hätte man die weißen Guts- und Plantagenbesitzer enteignen, massiv in Programme für Wohnen, Bildung und so weiter investieren müssen. Eine Auseinandersetzung mit der strukturellen Ungerechtigkeit, die aus unserer Geschichte herrührt, ist nie Bestandteil des amerikanischen Bewusstseins geworden. [...] Es gab viele Versuche, das zu tun. Aber der politische Wille hat nie ausgereicht. Der 200. Gründungstag der USA im Jahr 1976 wäre ein geeigneter Moment gewesen. Aber am Ende hatten wir eine komplette Spaltung des Gedenkens: Auf der einen Seite gab es nationalistische Feierlichkeiten[44], auf der anderen Seite standen die, die in Amerika den Quell allen Übels[45] sehen. Die Art, wie wir über Geschichte reden, ist leider eine Fortsetzung unserer polarisierten politischen Diskussion.
SPIEGEL: Kann man sagen, dass ein systemischer Rassismus[46] die amerikanische Gesellschaft durchzieht?
Lepore: Ja, auf jeden Fall mit Blick auf unser Strafsystem[47]. Man müsste sich intensiv mit der Frage befassen, warum unsere Rechtsordnung schwarze Männer kriminalisiert[48]. Weil das mühsam ist, redet man lieber über das persönliche Versagen Einzelner.
SPIEGEL: Hat der erste schwarze Präsident denn daran gar nichts geändert?
Lepore: Die Wahl von Barack Obama, und noch mehr seine Wiederwahl, waren ein historisch einschneidendes[49] Ereignis. Der Fehler war, dass viele gedacht haben, damit wäre das Kapitel Rassismus und Benachteiligung[50] in der amerikanischen Geschichte beendet. Das war leider nicht der Fall. [...]
SPIEGEL: Glauben Sie, dass ein wiedergewählter Trump Amerika in die Autokratie[51] führen wird?
Lepore: Trump führt die USA nirgendwohin, weil er gar nicht die Fähigkeit hat zu führen. Er wäre ein Autokrat, wenn er könnte. Aber seine eigene Inkompetenz macht ihm einen Strich durch die Rechnung[52].
SPIEGEL: Wie zuversichtlich sind Sie, dass ein neues, besseres Amerika aus dieser Krise hervorgehen wird?
Lepore: Ich habe große Sorgen, dass es nicht geschehen wird. Aber ich halte es für möglich. Es gibt mehr Anständigkeit[53] und guten Willen in Amerika, als derzeit sichtbar ist.
SPIEGEL: Frau Lepore, wir danken Ihnen für dieses Gespräch.

https://www.spiegel.de/politik/ausland/harvard-historikerin-ueber-den-fall-floyd-die-hierarchie-der-rassen-gehoert-zur-dna-des-landes-a-00000000-0002-0001-0000-000171426744, SPIEGEL 24/2020, 05.06.2020 [09.06.2020]

[36] to fuel sth. – [37] to judge sb./sth. – [38] disproportionately – [39] sovereignty of the people – [40] factual order/arrangement – [41] hierarchy of races – [42] heritage – [43] compensation – [44] nationalist celebrations – [45] root of all evil – [46] systemic racism – [47] penal system – [48] to criminalize sb. – [49] historically significant – [50] discrimination – [51] autocracy/absolute rule – [52] to thwart sb.'s plans – [53] decency

COMPREHENSION

M **1.** The interview can be divided roughly into three thematic units. First, read the interview. Then take notes in English on the aspects listed below:

1
- the U. S.'s loss of orientation and imbalance
- the influence and impact of the KKK
- the ongoing fight for freedom, equality and justice
- police brutality

2
- Black Power versus Black Lives Matter
- President Richard Nixon (1968)
- the presidency of Donald Trump
- the threat(s) to U. S. democracy

3
- the triple crisis
- racial hierarchy in the U. S.
- possible solutions
- the U. S. penal system
- the impact of Barack Obama
- President Trump's 'incompetence'

ACTIVITIES

2. Scenario:
Your school has an e-twinning project with a U. S. high school in which about 30 % of the students are African American. Of course, the killings of African Americans by white police officers have incited a lot of discussions and concerns. Your e-twin Matthew has asked you about the German perspective on all the incidents in the aftermath of the killing of George Floyd. He wants to know how the German media report on racism in the U. S.. Using your notes from task 1, write an email in which you

M
a) outline the *Spiegel* interview with Harvard historian Jill Lepore,
b) give a short overview of how the Black Lives Matter movement is seen in Germany,
c) tell him about your understanding of racism in Germany.

3. As in the U. S., many countries worldwide have had to deal with the crisis of the coronavirus pandemic and economic downturns – which as a tragic consequence hits poor sections of the population more than rich ones.
However, Lepore thinks that the U.S. might emerge from the crisis as a 'better' nation.
What is your view on the matter? Do you think that the U. S., the world … will be a better place after the crisis?
In a four-corners activity share and explain your views.

1 **The world will be a better place because …**

2 **Nothing will change at all because …**

4 **The world will be worse off because …**

3 **Some aspects will be better, e. g. …**

We the People! ... Still Living in a Nightmare Today

Ryan Nobles, Barbara Starr, Ryan Browne

1,600 Active-Duty Troops Sent to Washington Area After Some Governors Turn down Request for National Guard

AWARENESS

Read the Info box on p. 50 and find out about the killing of George Floyd in Minneapolis, and the demonstrations and violence it caused throughout the U. S. and worldwide.

The Pentagon[1] moved about 1,600 active-duty troops to the Washington area as the military is playing an increasing role in responding to protests in the nation's capital.

Pentagon chief spokesman Johnathan Hoffman said in a statement that the troops were sent from Fort Bragg in North Carolina and Fort Drum in New York. No active-duty forces have been deployed[2] in Washington to respond to the protests, which have gone on for five consecutive[3] nights in response to the death of George Floyd, a 46-year-old black man, in the custody[4] of Minneapolis police officers.

"Active duty elements are postured[5] on military bases in the National Capitol Region but are not in Washington, D. C.," Hoffman said in a statement. "They are on heightened alert[6] status but remain under Title X authority[7] and are not participating in defense support to civil authority operations."

The announcement came after Democratic governors in Virginia, New York, Pennsylvania and Delaware turned down requests from Defense Secretary Mark Esper to offer National Guard troops to help with security in Washington, D. C. Approximately 3,600 National Guard troops – 1,300 from Washington and 2,300 from other states – are currently in the capital, with 1,300 more guardsmen expected to arrive in the coming days, a US defense official told CNN.

In some instances, the Defense Department was counting on troop support from those states before the governors intervened.

"I can confirm that personnel from the NY National Guard were expected to move to D. C. last night, but permission was withdrawn by the governor," Lt. Col. Chris Mitchell, a Pentagon spokesman, said Tuesday morning.

During his daily press briefing, New York Gov. Andrew Cuomo said that New York's National Guard was completely focused on the state.

"I don't know what requests they've gotten, but I can tell you this, I wouldn't grant any request to send National Guard out of the state at this time because I want them in this state in case we need them," Cuomo said. [...]

Democratic Gov. John Carney's office confirmed to CNN that it received a request for troop help but decided against it because of the needs in Delaware, but also said the President's posture[8] played a role in the decision.

"Frankly the rhetoric out of the White House seemed like it had the potential to provoke additional unrest. For those reasons, the governor was not comfortable with members of the Delaware Guard assisting in the response. Delaware is not sending members of the Guard to Washington at this time," said Jonathan Starkey, Carney's deputy[9] chief of staff[10].

In Virginia, an official with a direct knowledge of the deliberations said Gov. Ralph Northam, a Democrat, made the decision not to send troops after consulting with Washington, D. C., Mayor Muriel Bowser and her office. [...]

In addition to being concerned about needing the troops in his own state to deal with violence in Virginia cities, Northam was also concerned about contributing to the response in Washington after President Donald Trump's call with governors on Monday, in which he lambasted[11] them over what he said were insufficient[12] responses to unrest in the wake[13] of George Floyd's death.

[1] **the Pentagon** building in Washington D. C. where the U. S. Defense Department is based – [2] **to deploy** *einsetzen, stationieren* – [3] **consecutive** following one after another without interruption – [4] **in the custody of** being kept under guard by – [5] **to posture** here: to place in position – [6] **alert** quick to act in a particular situation – [7] **Title X authority** law that defines the structure of the U. S. military – [8] **posture** attitude – [9] **deputy** *Stellvertreter* – [10] **chief of staff** an officer with very high rank in the armed forces – [11] **to lambast** to criticize sb./sth. severely – [12] **insufficient** no enough – [13] **in the wake of** happening after or because of sth.

"When it became clear that our troops would be under the command of the attorney general and not Mayor Bowser, we decided that it was not in our best interest to take part," the Virginia government official said. "The call with governors made it clear that the President was interested in escalating[14] the situation and the governor did not think that was responsible."

Pennsylvania state officials also confirmed that they, too, turned down the request out of concern for the need of troops to deal with issues in their state.

"Pennsylvania did receive this request. The National Guard currently has significant resources deployed across Pennsylvania. Their current priority is assisting commonwealth municipalities[15] in their response to de-escalate violence and keep our communities safe," said Lyndsay Kensinger, a spokeswoman for Pennsylvania Gov. Tom Wolf.

On Monday, Trump intensified his rhetoric about using military forces to "dominate" protesters and wished aloud there was an "occupying force"[16] in cities across America during a call with governors where he urged a tougher response to protests. Later, law enforcement officers fired what appeared to eyewitness accounts to be rubber bullets at a peaceful crowd outside the White House and smoke filled the air. A spokesman for the Pentagon told CNN Tuesday the National Guard did not fire tear gas or rubber bullets.

A group comprised of[17] service members who hold civilian jobs and train part-time, the National Guard are usually deployed in their home states by governors or the federal government who decide the length of each mission. They can perform law enforcement actions when under the command of state governors unlike the active military, which is forbidden by law from doing so unless the President invokes[18] the Insurrection Act[19].

https://edition.cnn.com/2020/06/02/politics/national-guard-states-pentagon/index.html, 3 June 2020 [06.06.2020]

Info

On 25 May, 46-year-old **George Floyd** was killed by Minneapolis police when an officer, Derek Chauvin, kneeled on his neck for nearly nine minutes. Floyd repeatedly said 'I can't breathe' but the four officers who had responded to the call, ignored his pleas and continued to restrain him. Paramedics were called in but could do nothing to help Floyd, who died of asphyxiation. He had been stopped by police for allegedly using a forged $20 note in a grocery store.

An eye-witness filmed the incident and the video went viral, sparking massive and immediate worldwide protests against police brutality and institutional racism. The four officers were fired the day after Floyd's death and were taken into custody and charged with murder soon after.

On June 5, the Minneapolis city council announced that police officers would no longer be allowed to use chokeholds and they would be required to intervene against any unauthorized use of force. The city council has also pledged to disband the city's police department and replace it with a new system of public safety. Outside experts will also be brought in to discuss how reforms can be implemented.

Adapted from: https://en.wikipedia.org/wiki/Killing_of_George_Floyd [06.06.2020]

COMPREHENSION

As in Germany, the U. S. police forces are primarily responsible for securing the peace and safety of the population. However, facing the wave of protests nationwide, the White House in Washington D. C. demanded that governors of the neighbouring states send troops to the capital.

1. After reading the article, take notes on how the various states and their governors reacted to the demand to send National Guard troops.

the Pentagon	**Virginia**	**New York (state)**
• sent 1,600 active duty troops • ...	• violence in cities ... • ...	• Gov. Cuomo: ... • ...
Pennsylvania	**Delaware**	
• ... • ...	• ... • ...	

[14] **to escalate** to make more serious – [15] **commonwealth municipality** a group of towns that have their own local government – [16] **occupying force** *Besatzungsmacht* – [17] **to be comprised of** (*fml.*) to consist of – [18] **to invoke** (*fml.*) to use a law in order to achieve sth. – [19] **Insurrection Act** a U. S. law from 1807 that empowers the president to deploy military and National Guard troops, e. g. to suppress civil disorder

2. Outline Delaware's Governor Carney's criticism of the White House and President Trump.

3. What were the concerns of Virginia and Pennsylvania state officials with regard to the President's rhetoric?

ANALYSIS

4. Read President Trump's tweets and explain how he wants the conflicts to be 'solved'.

1

Donald J. Trump
@realDonaldTrump

This Tweet violated the Twitter Rules about glorifying violence. However, Twitter has determined that it may be in the public's interest for the Tweet to remain accessible. Learn more

....These THUGS are dishonoring the memory of George Floyd, and I won't let that happen. Just spoke to Governor Tim Walz and told him that the Military is with him all the way. Any difficulty and we will assume control but, when the looting starts, the shooting starts. Thank you!

6:53 am · 29 May 2020 · Twitter for iPhone

2

Donald J. Trump
@realDonaldTrump

I can't stand back & watch this happen to a great American City, Minneapolis. A total lack of leadership. Either the very weak Radical Left Mayor, Jacob Frey, get his act together and bring the City under control, or I will send in the National Guard & get the job done right.....

6:53 vorm. · 29. Mai 2020 · Twitter for iPhone

5. (Re-)read the last paragraph of the article and explain the function of the National Guard. How are they different from the active military?

6. Team up with a partner and
a) describe the cartoons below in detail,
b) explain how the cartoonists view President Trump's way of handling the conflict

7. According to non-governmental civil rights organizations, 28 % of those killed by police since 2013 have been African Americans, although they make up only 13 % of the U.S. population. Between 1 January 2000 and 28 June 2019, there were 26,218 recorded deaths of people (of different ethnicities) during police interactions in the U. S. Some of the deaths of African Americans have become known to the public because of courageous witnesses who filmed the incidents and/or reported them to the media to highlight public outrage and encourage action.
Study the "Timeline of Deaths of African Americans Caused by Police" (p. 52) compiled by the BBC and compare the different cases.
What do the cases have in common and what differences can you detect?

Timeline of Deaths of African Americans Caused by Police

17 July 2014: Eric Garner

Eric Garner died after he was wrestled to the ground by a New York police officer on suspicion of illegally selling cigarettes. While in a choke hold, Mr Garner uttered the words "I can't breathe" 11 times. The incident – filmed by a bystander – led to protests across the country. The police officer involved was later fired, but was never prosecuted.

9 August 2014: Michael Brown

Michael Brown, 18, was killed by a police officer, in Ferguson, Missouri, who was responding to reports that Brown – who was not armed – had stolen a box of cigars. The exact circumstances of the encounter are disputed, but Brown was shot six times, according to autopsy reports. A report by the Department of Justice later concluded that the police force had displayed racial bias against Brown and used excessive force. The officer involved resigned from the force, but was not prosecuted.

22 November 2014: Tamir Rice

Tamir Rice, a boy of 12, was shot dead in Cleveland, Ohio by a police officer after reports of a male who was "probably a juvenile" pointing a gun that was "probably fake" at passers-by. Police claimed that they told Rice to drop the weapon – but instead of dropping it he pointed it at police. The police confirmed that the gun was a toy after Rice had been shot dead. There were no prosecutions after this case.

4 April 2015: Walter Scott

Walter Scott was shot in the back five times by a white police officer, who was later fired and eventually sentenced to 20 years in prison. Mr Scott had been pulled over for having a defective light on his car in North Charleston, South Carolina, and ran away from the police officer after a brief scuffle. The killing sparked protests in North Charleston, with chants of "No justice, no peace".

5 July 2016: Alton Sterling

Alton Sterling's death led to days of protests in Baton Rouge, Louisiana. Mr Sterling was killed after police responded to reports of a disturbance outside a shop. The incident was caught on mobile phone footage and spread online. The two officers involved did not face criminal charges, but one was dismissed and the other suspended from the police.

6 July 2016: Philando Castile

Philando Castile was killed while out driving with his girlfriend in St Paul, Minnesota. He was pulled over by the police during a routine check, and told them he was licensed to carry a weapon, and had one in his possession. He was shot as he was reaching for his licence, according to his girlfriend. She live-streamed the encounter on Facebook. The officer involved was cleared of murder charges.

18 March 2018: Stephon Clark

Stephon Clark died after being shot at least seven times in Sacramento, California, by police who were investigating a break-in. The district attorney said that the police had not committed a crime, as the officers said they feared for their lives believing Mr Clark was armed. Only a mobile phone was found at the scene.
The release of a police video of the incident sparked major protests in the city.

13 March 2020: Breonna Taylor

Breonna Taylor, a 26-year-old emergency medical technician was shot eight times when officers raided her apartment in Louisville, Kentucky. The police were executing a search warrant as part of a drugs raid, but no drugs were found. Louisville police said they returned fire after one officer was shot and wounded in the incident. The family has filed a lawsuit for wrongful death and excessive force. It says that Ms Taylor's partner fired in self-defence because the police did not identify themselves, and he believed they were being burgled.

25 May 2020: George Floyd

George Floyd dies after being arrested in Minneapolis, and held down by police officers, one of whom has his knee on Mr Floyd's neck. He pleaded that he couldn't breathe. Protests break out in cities across the US, and there are demonstrations in other parts of the world. One officer is charged with second-degree murder, and three others face charges of aiding and abetting murder.

https://www.bbc.com/news/world-us-canada-52905408 [10.06.2020]

ACTIVITIES

@ **8.** Do a project on killings and acts of violence during police interactions and research the websites below which present (interactive) maps and diagrams:
- https://fatalencounters.org/our-visualizations/
- https://mappingpoliceviolence.org

Prepare five-minute presentations to inform your class about your findings.

Former U.S.-Presidents' Reactions to George Floyd's Killing and the Trump Administration

AWARENESS

Do research on the three U.S. presidents Jimmy Carter, George W. Bush and Barack Obama and find out about their presidencies, political views and important events during their presidencies.

Jimmy Carter

Rosalynn and I are pained by the tragic racial injustices and consequent backlash[1] across our nation in recent weeks. Our hearts are with the victims' families and all who feel hopeless in the face of pervasive[2] racial discrimination and outright[3] cruelty. We all must shine a spotlight on the immorality of racial discrimination. But violence, whether spontaneous or consciously[4] incited[5], is not a solution.

As a white male of the South, I know all too well the impact of segregation and injustice to African Americans. As a politician, I felt a responsibility to bring equity[6] to my state and our country. In my 1971 inaugural address as Georgia's governor, I said: "The time for racial discrimination is over." With great sorrow and disappointment, I repeat those words today, nearly five decades later. Dehumanizing people debases[7] us all; humanity is beautifully and almost infinitely diverse. The bonds[8] of our common humanity must overcome the divisiveness[9] of our fears and prejudices.

Since leaving the White House in 1981, Rosalynn and I have strived to advance human rights in countries around the world. In this quest, we have seen that silence can be as deadly as violence. People of power, privilege, and moral conscience must stand up and say "no more" to a racially discriminatory police and justice system, immoral economic disparities[10] between whites and blacks, and government actions that undermine our unified[11] democracy. We are responsible for creating a world of peace and equality for ourselves and future generations.

We need a government as good as its people, and we are better than this.

https://www.cartercenter.org/news/pr/2020/statement-060320.html [07.08.2020]

George W. Bush

Laura and I are anguished[1] by the brutal suffocation[2] of George Floyd and disturbed by the injustice and fear that suffocate our country. Yet we have resisted the urge to speak out, because this is not the time for us to

[1] **backlash** reactions – [2] **pervasive** (*fml.*) present or noticeable in every part of a thing or place – [3] **outright** total – [4] **consciously** determined and intentional – [5] **to incite** to encourage sb. to do or feel sth. unpleasant or violent – [6] **equity** fairness, justice – [7] **to debase** to reduce the quality or value of sb./sth. – [8] **bond** sth. that unites people – [9] **divisiveness** disunity – [10] **disparity** inequality – [11] **unified** forming a single whole

[1] **anguished** having extreme mental suffering – [2] **suffocation** *Erstickung*

lecture. It is time for us to listen. It is time for America to examine our tragic failures – and as we do, we will also see some of our redeeming[3] strengths.

It remains a shocking failure that many African Americans, especially young African American men, are harassed[4] and threatened in their own country. It is a strength when protesters, protected by responsible law enforcement, march for a better future. This tragedy – in a long series of similar tragedies – raises a long overdue question: How do we end systemic racism in our society? The only way to see ourselves in a true light is to listen to the voices of so many who are hurting and grieving[5]. Those who set out to silence those voices do not understand the meaning of America – or how it becomes a better place.

America's greatest challenge has long been to unite people of very different backgrounds into a single nation of justice and opportunity. The doctrine and habits of racial superiority, which once nearly split our country, still threaten our Union. The answers to American problems are found by living up to American ideals – to the fundamental truth that all human beings are created equal and endowed by God with certain rights. We have often underestimated how radical that quest really is, and how our cherished[6] principles challenge systems of intended or assumed injustice. The heroes of America — from Frederick Douglass[7], to Harriet Tubman[8], to Abraham Lincoln, to Martin Luther King, Jr. – are heroes of unity. Their calling has never been for the fainthearted[9]. They often revealed the nation's disturbing bigotry[10] and exploitation – stains[11] on our character sometimes difficult for the American majority to examine. We can only see the reality of America's need by seeing it through the eyes of the threatened, oppressed, and disenfranchised[12].

That is exactly where we now stand. Many doubt the justice of our country, and with good reason. Black people see the repeated violation of their rights without an urgent and adequate response from American institutions. We know that lasting justice will only come by peaceful means. Looting[13] is not liberation[14], and destruction is not progress. But we also know that lasting peace in our communities requires truly equal justice. The rule of law ultimately depends on the fairness and legitimacy[15] of the legal system. And achieving justice for all is the duty of all.

This will require a consistent, courageous, and creative effort. We serve our neighbors best when we try to understand their experience. We love our neighbors as ourselves when we treat them as equals, in both protection and compassion. There is a better way – the way of empathy, and shared commitment, and bold[16] action, and a peace rooted in justice. I am confident that together, Americans will choose the better way.

https://twitter.com/TheBushCenter/status/1267933638454321154/photo/1 [07.08.2020]

Donald Trump's reaction to the Presidents' statements:

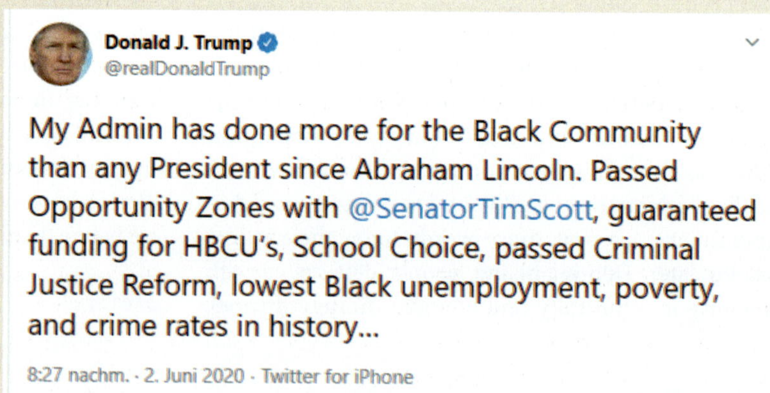
Donald J. Trump
@realDonaldTrump

My Admin has done more for the Black Community than any President since Abraham Lincoln. Passed Opportunity Zones with @SenatorTimScott, guaranteed funding for HBCU's, School Choice, passed Criminal Justice Reform, lowest Black unemployment, poverty, and crime rates in history...

8:27 nachm. · 2. Juni 2020 · Twitter for iPhone

[3] **redeeming** making sb./sth. seem less bad – [4] **to harass sb.** *jdn. schikanieren* – [5] **grieving** feeling very sad because sb. has died – [6] **to cherish** *verehren* – [7] **Frederick Douglass** (1818–1895) an African American social reformer, abolitionist, writer and statesman – [8] **Harriet Tubman** (ca. 1820–1913) African American abolitionist and social activist – [9] **fainthearted** not confident and brave and unwilling to take risks – [10] **bigotry** *Fanatismus* – [11] **stain** to leave a mark on sth. that is difficult to remove – [12] **disenfranchised** having no power to make people listen to your opinion or to affect the society you live in – [13] **looting** *Plündern* – [14] **liberation** the act ot helping sb. to be free – [15] **legitimacy** [lə'dʒɪtəməsi] the quality of being legal – [16] **bold** not frightened of danger

[1] **to pass sth.** *verabschieden* – [2] **opportunity zone** a U. S. investment programme allowing tax cuts etc. for people of lower income – [3] **HBCU** (*abbr.*) historically black colleges and universities

Barack Obama

[...] We can't forget that even as we're confronting the particular acts of violence that led to those losses, our nation and the world is still in the midst of a global pandemic that's exposed the vulnerabilities of our healthcare system, but also the disparate[1] treatment and, as a consequence the disparate impact that exists in our healthcare system, the unequal investment, the biases[2] that have led to a disproportionate number of infections and loss of life in communities of color. In a lot of ways, what has happened over the last several weeks is challenges and structural problems here in the United States have been thrown into high relief. They are the outcomes not just of the immediate moments in time, but they're the result of a long history of slavery and Jim Crow[3] and red lining[4] and institutionalized racism that too often have been the plague, the original sin of our society.

In some ways, as tragic as these past few weeks have been, as difficult and scary and uncertain as they've been, they've also been an incredible opportunity for people to be awakened to some of these underlying trends. They offer an opportunity for us to all work together to tackle them, to take them on, to change America and make it live up to its highest ideals.

[...]

Now I want to speak directly to the young men and women of color in this country, who [...] have witnessed too much violence and too much debt. Too often, some of that violence has come from folks who were supposed to be serving and protecting you. I want you to know that you matter. I want you to know that your lives matter, that your dreams matter. When I go home and I look at the faces of my daughters, Sasha and Malia, and I look at my nephews and nieces, I see limitless potential that deserves to flourish and thrive[5]. You should be able to learn and make mistakes and live a life of joy without having to worry about what's going to happen when you walk to the store or go for a jog or are driving down the street or looking at some birds in a park.

I hope that you also feel help hopeful, even as you may feel angry, because you have the power to make things better and you have helped to make the entire country feel as if this is something that's got to change. You've communicated a sense of urgency that is as powerful and as transformative as anything that I've seen in recent years.

I want to acknowledge[6] the folks in law enforcement that share the goals of re-imagining police, because there are folks out there who took their oath to serve your communities and your countries, have a tough job, and I know you're just as outraged about tragedies in recent weeks as are many of the protesters. We're grateful for the vast majority of you who protect and serve. I've been heartened[7] to see those in law enforcement who've recognized, let me march along with these protesters, let me stand side by side and recognize that I want to be part of the solution and who've shown restraint[8] and volunteered and engaged and listened, because you're a vital part of the conversation. Change is going to require everybody's participation. [...]

Very quickly, let me just close with a couple of specific things. What can we do?

Number one, we know there are specific evidence-based reforms that if we put in place today would build trust, save lives, would not show an increase in crime. Those are included in the 21st-century policing task force report. You can find it on Obama.org.

Number two, a lot of mayors and local elected officials read and supported the task force report, but then there wasn't enough follow through[9]. Today, I am urging every mayor in this country to review your use of force policies with members of your community and commit to report on planned reforms. What are the specific steps you can take?

I should add, by the way, that the original task force report was done several years ago. Since that time we've actually collected data, in part because we implemented some of these reform ideas, so we now have more information and more data as to what works. There are organizations like Campaign Zero and Color Of Change and others that are out there highlighting what the data shows, what works, what doesn't in terms of reducing incidents of police misconduct[10] and violence. Let's go ahead and start implementing those. We need mayors, county executives, others who are in positions of power to say this is a priority. This is a specific response.

[1] **disparate** (*fml.*) different in every way – [2] **bias** ['baɪəs] *Einseitigkeit, Vorurteil* – [3] **Jim Crow** the laws and policies once used in the U. S. to treat black people unfairly and to keep them apart from white people – [4] **red lining** the practice of refusing to lend money, give mortgages (*Hypothek*) or sell home insurance to people living in poor areas, or of charging them high rates for these services – [5] **to thrive** to do well – [6] **to acknowledge** to show that you are grateful – [7] **heartened** feeling happier and more positive about sth. – [8] **restraint** calm and controlled behaviour – [9] **follow through** action taken to complete a plan – [10] **misconduct** intentional bad behaviour

Number three, every city in this country should be a My Brother's Keeper community, because we have 250 cities, counties, tribal nations who are working to reduce the barriers and expand opportunity for boys and young men of color through programs and policy reforms, public private partnerships. Go to our website, get working with that, because it can make a difference. [...]

All right. Thank you, everybody. Proud of you guys. I know that we're going to be hearing from a bunch of people who have been on the front lines on this and know a lot more than I do about it. Proud of you.

https://www.rev.com/blog/transcripts/barack-obama-speech-transcript-on-george-floyd-death-protests [07.08.2020]

Tips on vocab

to be overweight ■ clothes that are too tight ■ to whistle ■ to have one's eyes closed ■ a box with White House props ■ to throw things away carelessly and without showing respect ■ the Bible ■ a copy of the U. S. Constitution ■ the U. S. flag ■ most important U. S. symbols are just used as accessories

Tips on vocab

a scene of horror and violence ■ the background lit with fire ■ black clouds of smoke ■ the President kneeling on Uncle Sam's neck ■ to have a pig's face and snout ■ to look like a pig ■ Uncle Sam lying on the ground ■ blood running from Uncle Sam's head ■ popping eyes ■ a masked man is kicking and beating Uncle Sam with a wooden slat ■ hoodie with the inscription ANTIFA (people who oppose fascism, often in a violent way)

1

2

COMPREHENSION

1. **Step 1:** Divide the class into three groups, with each group working with one of the presidents' statements.

   Step 2: After reading the texts, take notes on the respective aspects in the grid below and complete it.

president	personal concern	reference to history	reference to achievements during their presidency	looking into the future
Jimmy Carter	• a white male from the South • ...	• ...	• ...	• ...
George W. Bush	• ...	• Frederick Douglass • ...	• ...	• ...
Barack Obama	• African American • ...	• ...	• ...	• ...

   Step 3: The groups mix, exchange their results and complete the respective notes.

2. **All groups:** Read President Trump's tweet, which he posted in response to President Carter's and President Bush's remarks, and point out what he says about the achievements of his administration and presidency.

ANALYSIS

3. In your groups, examine the rhetorical and stylistic devices the presidents have employed in their statements. Pay particular attention to these aspects and how they are emphasized:
- encouragement, moral support, appeals
- positive and negative emotive words and word fields
- reproaches and accusations
- patterns of identification and solidarity and vice versa.

4. In groups, describe and analyse the cartoons on p. 56.
- What image of President Trump's abilities as president do the cartoons convey?
- Which of the president's attitudes and actions do they particularly criticize?

5. Relate your findings from task 4 to Article II of the U. S. Constitution (pp. 23 f.) in which the tasks and responsibilities of the president are described.

ACTIVITIES

6. "Hindsight is easier than foresight" (*Hinterher ist man immer schlauer*) is a common proverb used by somebody who is judged critically for their failures or mistakes by others. What is your opinion of the former presidents' remarks? Do you consider them to be helpful and appropriate or biased and unhelpful? Discuss your views in class.

@ **7.** What is your opinion of President Trump's tweet? Do research on what his administration "has done [...] for the Black Community" and find out whether (or not) his assertions are true.

Reactions to the Violent Protests

AWARENESS

Only hours after the video of George Floyd's killing went viral, tens of thousands of people, mostly organized by the Black Lives Matter movement, gathered in many U. S. cities to demonstrate against police brutality and racism. Sadly, the demonstrations weren't only peaceful; some turning violent with looting and vandalism, which resulted in Washington activating 62,000 National Guard troops. However, there were peaceful reactions as well, such as 12-year-old Keedron Bryant's song *I just want to live*, which he posted on Instagram and which got millions of likes.
- Find Keedron Bryant's original song on YouTube.
- Listen to the song and try to get an overall understanding of the lyrics and the message Keedron Bryant wants to convey.

1 Atlanta Mayor Keisha Lance Bottoms

Let me just speak to what's happening here today ... Above everything else, I am a mother. I am a mother to four Black children in America, one of whom is 18 years old. And when I saw the murder of George Floyd, I hurt like a mother would hurt. And on yesterday when I heard there were rumors about violent protests in Atlanta, I did what a mother would do: I called my son and I said, "Where are you?" I said, "I cannot protect you and Black boys shouldn't be out today."
So, you're not going to out-concern[1] me and out-care[2]

[1] **to out-concern sb.** to worry more intensely than sb. – [2] **to out-care sb.** to show or feel greater interest or anxiety than sb.

about where we are in America. I wear this each and every day, and I pray over my children each and every day. So what I see happening on the streets of Atlanta, is not Atlanta. This is not a protest. This is not in the spirit of Martin Luther King Jr. This is chaos. A protest has purpose: When Dr. King was assassinated, we didn't do this to our city.

So if you love this city ... This city that has had a legacy[3] of Black mayors, and Black police chiefs, and people who care about this city ... Where more than 50 % of the business owners in Metro[4] Atlanta are minority business owners ... If you care about this city, then go home. And pray that somebody like Reverend Beasley[5] will come and talk to you and give you some instructions on what a protest should look like, and how you effectuate change in America. This police chief made a video on yesterday – pull it up on YouTube – where she said she was appalled[6] to watch the murder of George Floyd. This woman did that. You're not honoring the legacy of Martin Luther King Jr. and the Civil Rights Movement; you are not protesting anything running out with brown liquor[7] in your hands, breaking windows in this city. T.I.[8], Killer Mike[9] owned half the West side, so when you burn down this city, you're burning down our community.

If you want change in America go and register to vote. Show up at the polls on June 9th[10]. Do it in November[11]. That is the change we need in this country. You are disgracing our city, you are disgracing the life of George Floyd and every other person who has been killed in this country. We are better than this. We are better than this as a city. We are better than this as a country.

Go home. Go home. In the same way I couldn't protect my son on yesterday, I cannot protect you out in those streets. You are throwing knives at our police officers, you are burning cars. You have defaced[12] the CNN[13] building. Ted Turner[14] started CNN in Atlanta 40 years ago because he believed in who we are as a city. There was a Black reporter who was arrested on camera this morning who works for CNN. They are telling our stories. And you are disgracing their building.

This is not the legacy of civil rights in America. This is chaos, and we are buying into[15] it. This won't change anything. We're no longer talking about the murder of an innocent man. We're talking about how you're burning police cars on the streets of Atlanta, Georgia.

Go home.

11 Alive, transcript: Lucy Buxton, https://www.youtube.com/watch?v=O7z6m2os2g, 30 May 2020 [09.09.2020]

2 NYC Top Cop Apologizes for NYPD's 'Part in Racial Bias'

New York City's top cop called for calm amid[1] days of protests and unrest across New York City, and also apologized on behalf of the department for the NYPD's "part in racial bias."

Along with peaceful demonstrations, there have been smash-and-grab[2] sprees[3] and a string[4] of assaults on police officers in the wake of[5] the death of George Floyd. The stabbing[6] of an officer in Brooklyn Wednesday was one of multiple assaults on police officers in recent days, including a driver plowing into[7] a sergeant in the Bronx, a lieutenant struck in the helmet by a brick during a brawl[8] in Manhattan, a Molotov cocktail thrown into a van full of officers in Brooklyn, and gunshots fired at an occupied police cruiser in Queens.

At the same time, police have been criticized for harsh tactics to corral[9] protesters and enforce the curfew[10].

[3] **legacy** ['legəsi] sth. that is part of your history – [4] **metro** relating to a large city and the area surrounding it – [5] **Reverend Beasley** (*1936) African American civil rights leader and activist – [6] **appalled** *angewidert* – [7] **brown** liquor brown-coloured alcoholic beverage like whiskey – [8] **T. I.** name of a Southern rapper, nicknamed 'King of Dirty South' – [9] **Killer Mike** an African American rapper, writer, actor and activist – [10] **June 9th** day of election of the nominated candidates for the presidential election; *Vorwahlen* – [11] **November** month in which the presidential election takes place; here: 3 November 2020 – [12] **to deface** to damage and spoil the appearance of something by writing or drawing on it – [13] **CNN** (*abbr.*) Cable News Network: a US organization that broadcasts news on television internationally – [14] **Ted Turner** (*1938) U. S. media magnate, TV producer and philanthropist; founder of CNN (1980) – [15] **to buy into sth.** (*phr. v.*) to completely believe in a set of ideas

[1] **amid** in the middle of or surrounded by – [2] **smash-and-grab** a crime in which thieves break the window of a shop and steal things before quickly escaping – [3] **spree** a period of wild irresponsible behaviour – [4] **string** a set of events following each other closely – [5] **in the wake of** happening after and sometimes because of sth. – [6] **to stab sb.** *jdn. erstechen* – [7] **to plow into** (*phr. v.*) to hit sb./sth. with great force – [8] **brawl** a noisy, rough and uncontrolled fight – [9] **to corral sb.** to bring a group of people together and keep them in one place, especially in order to control them – [10] **curfew** *Ausgangs-sperre*

More than 350 current and former members of Mayor Bill de Blasio's administration published an open letter Thursday denouncing[11] brutality, such as officers swatting[12] protesters with batons[13], a police vehicle driven into a crowd and an officer seen throwing a woman to the ground.

Commissioner Dermot Shea spoke at a news conference Thursday that opened with a broadside[14] against elected officials and others whom he blamed for stirring up animosity[15] by speaking against police and sharing videos on social media that, presented without context, are seen as evidence of officer misconduct[16].

He said use of force is often justified, but that the NYPD is reviewing about seven instances that may result in discipline. Shea said without a doubt, there will be a couple of officers suspended.

"Before you start commenting on a six-second video do a little homework," Shea said.

But the commissioner continued to apologize for what he referred to as many other mistakes.

"Sometimes even the best, and the NYPD is the God d***[17] best police department in this country, but sometimes even the best fall down. So for our part, and the damage to civility, for our part in racial bias, in excessive force, unacceptable behavior, unacceptable language, and many other mistakes ... we are human ... I am sorry. Are you?"

Shea said the department has worked to fundamentally change policing over the last seven years, including reducing arrests and summonses and increasing training.

"How do we move forward?" Shea said. "I do not know how we will get there. I wish I had all the answers, but I know this much. We cannot reach that place until we end the hateful speech and the law breaking and the unprovoked attacks against police officers and the rhetoric that fuels[18]."

https://abc7ny.com/nypd-apology-police-commissioner-dermot-shea-nyc-curfew-aftermath/6232175/, 5 June 2020 [04.06.2020]

1

Police officers kneel in Coral Gables, Florida

2

U.S. Speaker of the House Nancy Pelosi and Democratic lawmakers kneel at the Capitol's Emancipation Hall for 8 minutes 46 seconds for George Floyd, 8 June 2020. Emancipation Hall is named in memory of the enslaved workers who helped to build the U.S. Capitol.

COMPREHENSION

In contrast to President Trump's aggressive and polarizing rhetoric, many political officials and police representatives tried to de-escalate the situation and appealed to people's reason and sense of community.

1. One of the first officials to talk to the public was Atlanta Mayor Keisha Lance Bottoms. Read her TV speech and point out
- what she reveals about her private life
- how she appeals to people's sense of responsibility
- what she says about the civil rights movement and Martin Luther King
- how she describes CNN and its role.

[11] **to denounce** to criticize sb./sth. strongly and publicly – [12] **to swat** to hit something hard by suddenly using your hand or an object – [13] **baton** a thick, heavy stick used as a weapon by police officers – [14] **broadside** a forceful spoken or written attack – [15] **animosity** *Feindseligkeit* – [16] **misconduct** *Fehlverhalten* – [17] **d***** damned – [18] **to fuel sth.** *etw. anheizen*

2. New York's 'top cop', police commissioner Dermot Shea, gave a statement on TV to explain the difficult situation.
   - Give an outline of the various violent incidents NYPD police officers had to deal with.
   - How does Shea explain (or justify) the mistakes the police made?
   - What are Shea's plans for the future?

ANALYSIS

3. Examine Keisha Lance Bottoms' persuasive strategy and explain which stylistic means and rhetorical devices she uses to evoke sympathy and compassion in the listeners but appeal to their responsibility as well.

4. Explain Commissioner Dermot Shea's strategy of apologizing for "racial bias" on the one hand but asking the listeners if they were "sorry" as well and "doing [their] homework".

ACTIVITIES

5. In 2016, Colin Kaepernick, quarterback for the San Francisco 49ers, knelt during the national anthem before games to protest against racial inequality and police brutality against people of colour. Since then, 'taking a knee' or 'kneeling down' has become an expression of solidarity.
   @ Take a look at the photos on p. 59 and research the various acts of kneeling in the wake of the killing of George Floyd. What were the police officers'/politicians' intention and motivation for doing so and what was the public reaction to these acts of kneeling?

6. In her TV speech, Mayor Keisha Lance Bottoms says, "If you want change in America, go and register to vote. Show up at the polls. [...]. This is the change we need in this country." (ll. 38 ff.)
   In a four-corners activity, express your opinion of this statement.

1 **Voting is a waste of time ... politicians don't listen ...**	2 **Voting and elections are the essence of democracy ...**
4 **Demonstrating is more effective than voting ...**	3 **Voting often only involves 50 % ... it's very frustrating ...**

And Meanwhile ... the President of the United States ...

AWARENESS

In the wake of the killing of George Floyd, demonstrations and riots of outraged Americans took place in more then 2,000 U. S. cities. In Washington D. C., there were thousands of protesters in front of the White House demanding change. If you were the president or one of his advisory staff, what would you do (or recommend the president to do) to calm down the public and de-escalate the situation?

1 Peter Beaumont: Trump Fled to Bunker as Protests over George Floyd Raged[1] outside the White House

Donald Trump was taken to the secure White House bunker, usually reserved for times of war or terrorist attacks, in the midst of noisy protests on Friday about the killing of George Floyd by police, and sporadic[2] clashes close to the presidential complex's perimeter[3].

According to several accounts by unnamed officials, Trump spent nearly an hour sequestered[4] in the austere[5] suite of hardened underground rooms designed for use in grave[6] emergencies, and in which the then vice-president, Dick Cheney[7], took shelter during the 9/11 attacks.

The decision to move the president to the bunker was attributed to US Secret Service officers tasked with protecting him. It was taken as chants[8] from protesters in nearby Lafayette Park could be heard in the White House, and Secret Service and DC and park police were required to push back demonstrators from barriers close to the White House, some of whom were throwing stones and water bottles.

The decision to take Trump to the bunker, first reported in the New York Times, preceded[9] the turning off of external lights at the White House during further protests on Sunday, and has inevitably[10] reinforced[11] the sense of a president under siege[12].

Largely unheard from except for the stream of predictably[13] accusatory[14] and inflammatory[15] tweets, Trump did, however, condemn Floyd's killing in a speech marking[16] the SpaceX[17] launch in Florida on Saturday.

The White House and Secret Service remarked that they did not comment on security protocols and decisions or the means and methods of protective operations. The bunker is hardened to withstand the force of a passenger jet crashing into the White House.

The incident provoked a stream of derisive[18] comments on social media, comparing Trump unfavourably both to the presumptive[19] Democratic candidate, Joe Biden, who visited protesters and to the cowardly lion[20] from the Wizard of Oz[21]. The hashtag "#bunkerboy" became a trending term on Twitter.

[...]

Colin Hanks, the actor son of Tom Hanks, described the incident as a metaphor for Trump's presidency. "Trump is not a leader. He KNOWS it in his bones. He is a coward. Turning off the lights, pretending no one is home while hiding in a bunker. There is no better metaphor for his, and his entire administration's failures. The election is in seven months. VOTE. HIM. OUT."

Trump, who has tweeted encouraging the use of lethal[22] force against "looters", and warned protesters outside the White House of "vicious[23] dogs" and "ominous[24] weapons", has told advisers he worries about his safety, while both privately and publicly praising the work of the Secret Service.

By Monday Trump was calling for "law and order" and blaming far-left agitators for a sixth straight night of violent nationwide protests.

After his visit to the Space X Launch in Florida on Saturday, Trump returned to a White House under virtual siege, with protesters, some violent, gathered just a

[1] **to rage** to happen in a strong or violent way – [2] **sporadic** happening sometimes – [3] **perimeter** the outer edge of an area of land – [4] **sequestered** quiet and hidden from other people – [5] **austere** plain and without unnecessary details – [6] **grave** seriously bad – [7] **Dick (Richard) Cheney** (*1941) American politician and U. S. Vice President (2001 – 2009) – [8] **chant** word or phrase that is repeated many times – [9] **to precede** to be before sth. in time – [10] **inevitably** *unausweichlich* – [11] **to reinforce** to make sth. stronger – [12] **siege** *Belagerung* – [13] **predictably** *vorhersagbar* – [14] **accusatory** *beschuldigend* – [15] **inflammatory** *anheizend* – [16] **marking sth.** *aus Anlass von etw.* – [17] **SpaceX** U. S. aerospace manufacturer and space transportation services company founded by Elon Musk – [18] **derisive** (*fml.*) *spöttisch, verächtlich* – [19] **presumptive** (*fml.*) *mutmaßlich* – [20] **cowardly lion** a character in the fictional Land of Oz – [21] **The Wizard of Oz** American children's novel (1900) by L. Frank Baum – [22] **lethal** causing death; extremely dangerous – [23] **vicious** intending to hurt badly; likely to be violent – [24] **ominous** here: very dangerous

few hundred yards away through much of the night. Demonstrators returned on Sunday afternoon, facing off[25] against police at Lafayette Park into the evening. [...]

Trump has been widely criticized for his response to the protests that have rocked[26] the nation since video of Floyd's death began spreading on social media.

Despite days of peaceful protests and violent clashes with police in some of America's major cities, Trump has not addressed the nation and has repeatedly sent inflammatory messages over Twitter.

Late on Friday, Trump tweeted that protesters could have been attacked with dogs and weapons wielded[27] by the US Secret Service and accused the DC mayor for supposedly not providing police to protect the White House.

"They let the 'protesters' scream and rant[28] as much as they wanted, but whenever someone got too frisky[29] or out of line, they would quickly come down on them, hard – didn't know what hit them," Trump said.

"If they had [breached[30] the fence]," the president continued, "they would have been greeted with the most vicious dogs, and most ominous weapons, I have ever seen. That's when people would have been really badly hurt, at least."

The president has spoken to George Floyd's grieving[31] family, but, according to Floyd's brother Philonise Floyd, the conversation was brief. "He didn't give me an opportunity to even speak," Floyd told MSNBC[32].

 https://www.theguardian.com/us-news/2020/may/31/trump-flees-to-bunker-as-protests-over-george-floyd-rage-outside-white-house [06.06.2020]

2 Martin Pengelly: Trump Claims He Was in Bunker for a 'Tiny' Period of Time to Inspect It

[...] Trump earned rebukes[1] on Saturday by tweeting that had protesters breached the White House fence, they would have been met by "vicious dogs" and "ominous weapons".

The protests in Washington and cities across the country, the worst civil unrest since the assassination of Martin Luther King Jr in 1968, arose from the killing in Minneapolis last week of George Floyd, a 46-year-old African American man who died after a police officer kneeled on his neck for almost nine minutes.

"After we had the one evening which was a little rough," Trump told [Brian] Kilmeade [a Fox News host], "we brought in the troops".

In a call on Monday which was leaked to outlets[2] including the Guardian, Trump harangued[3] governors about the need to "dominate" protesters, and demanded they call in the national guard. Guardsmen and federal officers have been deployed[4] in Washington. On Tuesday, soldiers of the regular US army were moved within reach of the capital.

Kilmeade asked Trump if, as was reported, the Secret Service had told him he had to "go downstairs" in order to protect his welfare.

"No, they didn't tell me that at all," the president said, "but they said it would be a good time to go down, to take a look, because maybe some time you're going to need it ... I looked, I was down for a very, very short period of time ... a whole group of people went with me, as an inspecting factor."

President Trump in front of Ashburton House, the parish house of St. John's Episcopal Church

[25] **to face off against** *es auf eine Machtprobe mit jdm. ankommen lassen* – [26] **to rock** to cause feelings of shock – [27] **to wield** to hold a weapon or tool and look as if you are going to use it – [28] **to rant** to speak or shout in a loud and uncontrolled way often saying confused or silly things – [29] **frisky** (*infml.*) full of activity – [30] **to breach** (*fml.*) to break an opening into sth. – [31] **grieving** feeling very sad because sb. has died – [32] **MSNBC** (*abbr.*) Microsoft National Broadcasting Company; American news-based pay TV channel

[1] **rebuke** (*fml.*) *Zurechtweisung* – [2] **outlet** newspaper, TV station, website, etc. that makes information or other services available to the public – [3] **to harangue** [həˈræŋ] *jdm. Vorhaltungen machen* – [4] **to deploy** to move soldiers and equipment to where they are needed

It was reported at the weekend that the first lady, Melania Trump, and the president's son Barron Trump also went to the bunker.

"And, Brian, it was during the day," Trump insisted, "it wasn't during the night. I think they reported during the night. During the night, maybe some day it makes sense." [...]

Extensive reporting citing administration officials said Trump wanted to make the walk – and therefore precipitated[5] the assault with rubber bullets and chemical agents[6] on peaceful protesters including priests, a hugely controversial move – to counter the perception he had hidden in the bunker on Friday.

The decision to use the historic "Church of the Presidents" for such a photo op[7] attracted widespread criticism, including from religious leaders. Some Trump supporters expressed approval.

Trump insisted: "Most religious leaders loved it. I heard [evangelical leader] Franklin Graham this morning thought it was great, I heard many other people think it was great ... it was only the other side that didn't like it." [...] The church was boarded up when Trump arrived. [...]

3 Maegan Vazquez: Trump Invokes[1] Floyd's Name While Taking Economic Victory Lap[2]

President Donald Trump invoked George Floyd's name during a Friday bill signing ceremony touting[3] the latest jobs report, which exceeded[4] economists' expectations.

"We all saw what happened last week. We can't let that happen. Hopefully George is looking down and saying this is a great thing that's happening for our country. (It's) a great day for him. It's a great day for everybody," Trump said during a White House Rose Garden event before signing a piece of legislation devoted to small business loan[5] flexibility.

"This is a great, great day in terms of equality," Trump added.

Floyd's death in police custody[6] has sparked[7] massive, mostly peaceful protests across the country. Despite the arrests of all four officers involved, protests have continued over issues of systemic racism and police brutality.

Trump's comment about Floyd "looking down" was introduced by unwieldy[8] and unprepared remarks, in which he devoted a significant portion to praising the job law enforcement was doing to quell[9] demonstrators and urging some states to activate the National Guard. Speaking in reference to Floyd, Trump maintained that "equal justice under the law must mean that every American receives equal treatment in every encounter with law enforcement regardless of race, color, gender or creed[10]. They have to receive fair treatment from law enforcement."

But at no point did Trump explicitly[11] bring up whether the source of that problem – a lack of just treatment by law enforcement – was systemic racism. In fact, Trump reiterated[12] the need to "dominate" any violent protesters, despite rising concern in cities across the nation about violent arrests and alleged[13] assaults by police on demonstrators.

And as protesters in the wake of Floyd's death continue across the country to demand racial equality and policing reform, Trump's solution has been to, once again, campaign by crediting[14] his administration's efforts to boost the economy.

When Trump sat down to sign the bill, the PPP Flexibility Act[15], he shushed[16] reporters trying to ask him questions.

"What's happened to our country and what you now see, it's been happening, is the greatest thing that can happen for race relations, for the African American community, for the Asian American (community), for the Hispanic American community, for women, for

[5] **to precipitate** to make sth. happen suddenly or sooner than expected – [6] **chemical agent** *chemischer Wirkstoff* – [7] **photo op** (*infml.*) photo opportunity; an occasion when a politician or famous person is photographed doing something that will make them popular with the public

[1] **to invoke** (*fml.*) *anführen, beschwören* – [2] **victory lap** *Ehrenrunde des Siegers* – [3] **to tout** [taʊt] to praise greatly – [4] **to exceed** to be greater than – [5] **loan** *Darlehen* – [6] **custody** *Obhut, Gewahrsam* – [7] **to spark** to cause the start of sth. – [8] **unwieldy** *schwerfällig, plump* – [9] **to quell** to stop sth., esp. by using force – [10] **creed** (*fml.*) a system of beliefs or principles – [11] **explicitly** in a way that is clear and exact – [12] **to reiterate** (*fml.*) to repeat – [13] **alleged** *angeblich* – [14] **to credit** to praise or recognize achievement – [15] **PPP Flexibility Act** (*abbr.*) Paycheck Protection Program Flexibility Act; a system that gives companies more time to spend loan funds and to spend less on payroll – [16] **to shush sb.** (*infml.*) to tell sb. to be quiet

everything – because our country is so strong and that's what my plan is," Trump said before signing the bill.

The President did not answer questions about Asian American and African American unemployment, which was less robust than other minority groups.

For the second month in a row, fewer than half of black Americans were working, with only 49.6% of the population employed, up less than 1 percentage point from April. The last time such a small share were working was in 1983. [...]

https://edition.cnn.com/2020/06/05/politics/donald-trump-george-floyd-rose-garden/index.html [06.06.2020]

Tips on vocab

a scene of chaos, horror and violence ■ approaching soldiers wearing combat gear and gas masks ■ machine guns ■ billowing flames in the background ■ African Americans wearing masks are trampled down ■ allusion to the victims of the coronavirus ■ an obese orange figure draped in the U.S. flag resembling President Trump is leading the troops ■ to hold up a Bible ■ the top part of his head opens with a flap and steam is coming out ■ the White House seems to be on fire

COMPREHENSION

1. Read the **first article** and describe
   - why President Trump was moved to the bunker
   - how people reacted to Trump's stay in the bunker
   - Trump's reaction to the demonstrating crowds.

2. Give an outline of the **second article** and what it reports about
   - Trump's threats, justifications and explanations
   - Trump's "photo op" in front of the church.

3. As Trump was criticized for not showing any empathy and for even worsening the situation, he tried to gloss over the critical situation. Read the **third article**, published by American broadcasting giant CNN, and give details of Trump's various attempts to
   - show that his administration is in control of the situation
   - emphasize his success and achievements
   - refer to George Floyd.

ANALYSIS

4. Divide the class into three groups, with each group working with one of the articles. Explain how the British and U. S. journalists directly and indirectly express their criticism of President Trump and his administration. Examine the journalists'
   - choice of words and
   - means employed to appear credible.

5. Describe the photograph of President Trump on p. 62 and explain how the different details are intended to support the image of the president's strength and credibility.
   What overall impression does the photo convey?

6. Look at the cartoon on p. 64, which was inspired by the famous painting *Liberty Leading the People* by Eugène Delacroix commemorating the July Revolution of 1830 in Paris, leading to the removal of Charles X from the throne.
   Describe the various details of the cartoon and explain its message.

7. The photo shows National Guard troops on the steps of the Lincoln Memorial in Washington D. C.

   Step 1:
   @ Do research on the Lincoln Memorial and what it stands for.

   Step 2:
   The photo conveys different messages, depending on which (political) side you are on.
   a) Explain the intended messages to the protesters as seen from the Trump administration's perspective.
   b) Explain the photo's message as perceived from the protesters' perspective.

   What is the problem about the clashing perspectives and how could it possibly be solved?

National Guard troops standing on the steps of the Lincoln Memorial in Washington, D. C.

Tips on vocab

soldiers wearing (camouflage) combat gear ■ helmets ■ sunglasses ■ dark masks ■ to stand at a distance from each other ■ to appear emotionless ■ pillars of the Lincoln Memorial ■ to resemble a Greek temple

ACTIVITIES

8. Imagine you are one of the men or women standing guard at the Lincoln Memorial. What might they be thinking?
   Write an interior monologue that reflects possible anger, fear, concern, etc.
   Then, read out your monologues in class and discuss the different thoughts and ideas.

Anne Applebaum

The Rest of the World Is Laughing at Trump

AWARENESS

Step 1:

@ Find out the meaning of the words and expressions below.

laughing stock ● Aunt Sally ● blockhead ● butt ● everybody's fool ● ignoramus ● dupe ● target ● dunkhead ● mockery ● figure of fun ● bubblehead ● sport ● buffoon

Step 2:

Trump's behaviour and especially his rhetoric have been a good source of material for the media and for cartoonists in particular.

M Describe the cartoons below in detail, paying particular attention to textual and visual elements, and explain what picture they draw of the president's capabilities.

Dressierter Kakadu übernimmt US-Präsidentschaft.

VIRTUAL REALITY oder: MASKENTRAGEN IM WEISSEN HAUS ...

Tips on vocab

the Oval Office in the White House ■ trained cockatoo ■ white feathers ■ yellow head feathers ■ to sit at the president's desk ■ to parrot (*nachplappern*) ■ to repeat things parrot-fashion

Tips on vocab

to roam around (*umherirren*) ■ the Oval Office in the White House ■ to wear virtual reality glasses ■ to brawl (*rumkrakeelen*) ■ extinction of the mob ■ to make a song and dance about it (*idm., viel Trara um etw. machen*)

The president created a leadership vacuum. China intends to fill it. [...]

Propaganda [...] works best in a vacuum, when there are no competing messages, or when the available alternative messengers inspire no trust. Since mid-March, China has been sending messages out into precisely this kind of vacuum: a world that has been profoundly[1] changed not just by the virus, but by the American president's simultaneously[2] catastrophic and ridiculous failure to cope with it. [...]

The incredulous[3] first paragraph of an article in Sowetan, from South Africa, declares that "US President Donald Trump has again left people stunned[4] and confused with his bizarre suggestion that disinfectant and ultraviolet light could possibly be used to treat Covid-19." [...]

Quotations from the president's astonishing April 23 press conference have appeared on every continent, via countless television channels, radio stations, magazines, and websites, in hundreds of thousands of variations and dozens of languages – often accompanied by

[1] **profoundly** deeply or extremely – [2] **simultaneously** happening at exactly the same time – [3] **incredulous** *ungläubig* – [4] **stunned** shocked

warnings, in case someone was fooled, not to drink disinfectant or bleach. In years past, many of these outlets presumably[5] published articles critical of this or that aspect of U.S. foreign policy, blaming one U.S. president or another. But the kind of coverage we see now is something new. This time, people are not attacking the president of the United States. They are laughing at him. Beppe Severgnini, one of Italy's best-known columnists, told me that while Italians feel enormous empathy for Americans who have suffered as they have, they feel differently about Trump: "In this time of darkness and depression, he keeps us entertained." [...]

This time, Americans are doing ... nothing. Or to be more specific, because plenty of American governors, mayors, doctors, scientists, and tech companies are doing things, the White House is doing nothing. There is no presidential leadership inside the United States; there is no American leadership in the world. Members of the G7[6] – the U.S. and its six closest allies – did meet to write a joint[7] statement. But even that tepid[8] project ended in ludicrous[9] rancor[10] when the American secretary of state, Mike Pompeo, insisted on using the expression "Wuhan virus" and the others gave up in disgust. Not only is the president talking nonsense, not only is America absent, but the nation's top diplomat is a caricature of a tough guy – someone who throws around insults[11] in the absence of any capacity to influence events.

Others are drawing even more radical conclusions, and with remarkable speed. The "disinfectant" comments – and the laughter that followed – mark not so much a turning point as an acceleration[12] point, the moment when a transformation that began much earlier suddenly started to seem unstoppable. Although we are still only weeks into this pandemic, although the true scale of the health crisis and the economic catastrophe[13] is still unknown, the outline of a very different, post-American, post-coronavirus world is already taking shape. It's a world in which American opinions will count less, while the opinions of America's rivals will count more. And that will change political dynamics in ways that Americans haven't yet understood. [...]

Chinese propaganda may find unexpectedly fertile[14] ground elsewhere too. Chinese aid has also been delivered to Japan and South Korea, two U.S. allies who have sought close relationships with Trump and have received, in exchange, demands that they pay more for American bases. As close neighbors and former foes[15], both countries have many reasons to be wary[16] of China. But now that Trump is a laughing stock[17], now that America is absent from the game, some in both Tokyo and Seoul may conclude that they should start hedging bets[18]. [...]

China's relationships with the Arab world have also deepened during the pandemic. Qatar, Saudi Arabia, and Kuwait sent aid to Wuhan during the earlier part of the crisis; later, China reciprocated[19]. The foreign minister of the United Arab Emirates has described China as the role model to follow in this crisis. On March 8, Chinese medical workers arrived in Baghdad – an advance team, perhaps, poised[20] to take advantage of the inevitable American retreat. In each one of these places, America is absent, distracted[21], stumbling[22] – and laughable.

To be absolutely crystal clear: I am not praising China's efforts. I am simply calling attention to the fact that, in a world where people laugh at the American president, they might succeed. Inside the bubble of officials who surround Pompeo, it may well seem very brave and cutting-edge[23] to use the expression "Wuhan virus" or to call for bigger and bolder rhetorical attacks on China. But out there in the real world – out there in the world where Pompeo's boss is perceived as a sinister clown, and Pompeo himself as just the sinister[24] clown's lackey[25] – not very many people are listening. Once again: A vacuum has opened up, and the Chinese regime is leading the race to fill it. [...]

We are no longer a serious nation. We are as ignorant as our thoughtless, narcissistic[26], ignorant president. Don't be surprised if the rest of the world takes note of that, too.

https://www.theatlantic.com/ideas/archive/2020/05/time-americans-are-doing-nothing/611056/, 3 May 2020 [10.06.2020]

[5] **presumably** *vermutlich, wahrscheinlich* – [6] **G7** the Group of Seven; an international economic organization consisting of Canada, France, Germany, Italy, Japan, the U.K. and the U.S. – [7] **joint** shared between two or more people – [8] **tepid** not enthusiastic – [9] **ludicrous** stupid or unreasonable and deserving to be laughed at – [10] **rancor** (*US, fml.*) *Groll* – [11] **insult** *Beleidigung* – [12] **acceleration** the increase in speed – [13] **catastrophe** [kəˈtæstrəfi] – [14] **fertile ground for sth.** (*idm.*) a situation or place that produces good results or a lot of ideas – [15] **foe** enemy – [16] **wary** not completely trusting sb./sth. – [17] **laughing stock** *Lachnummer, Witzfigur* – [18] **to hedge your bets** (*idm.*) *auf Nummer sicher gehen* – [19] **to reciprocate** to do or give sth. in return – [20] **poised** ready to do sth. at any moment – [21] **distracted** nervous or confused – [22] **to stumble** to walk in a way that does not seem controlled – [23] **cutting-edge** very modern and with all the newest features – [24] **sinister** evil, or suggesting that sth. evil is going to happen – [25] **lackey** (*disapproving*) *Laufbursche, Lakai* – [26] **narcissistic** (*disapproving*) having too much interest in and admiration for oneself

COMPREHENSION

Anne Applebaum (*1964) is a Pulitzer Prize-winning American journalist and historian writing for *The Atlantic*, a literary and cultural commentary magazine which is considered to be one of the top English-language magazines. The March 2019 cover article formally called for the impeachment of Donald Trump.

1. After reading the article, complete the following sentences with evidence from the text:
   a) China has been able to send messages of leadership to the world because …
   b) President Trump suggested to the American people to treat Covid-19 by …
   c) The international reaction to President Trump's suggestions was …
   d) The Italians differentiate between Trump and the American people and …
   e) The White House is doing nothing which means that …
   f) The G7 states were unable to reach an agreement because …
   g) American opinions count less today because …
   h) The post-American, post-coronavirus world will change and …
   i) During the coronavirus pandemic, China supported many countries worldwide by …
   j) Instead of helping and leading, the U. S. …
   k) In the real world, Trump and his staff are perceived as …

2. Point out why the author is convinced that China is the leading nation in the global race to fill the vacuum that the U. S. has created.

3. Present the author's concluding view of the U. S. as a nation.

ANALYSIS

4. Examine the author's compelling line of argument and train of thought and explain how she aims at appealing to the reader.

5. Analyse the use of rhetorical devices, focusing on the use of
   - the (positive and negative) choice of words
   - contrast (antithesis)
   - repetition and enumeration
   - climax.

ACTIVITIES

6. The author criticizes that America is losing/has already lost its leadership role in the world – and that China is taking over.
   Discuss
   a) whether (or not) you think this fear is justified and
   b) what possible dangers this loss might bring about.

Guido Mingels et al.

The Last Stand[1]: Trump's Handling of the Coronavirus Could Cost Him Presidency

AWARENESS

> "[...] every single one of us has a God-given power, and [...] the fate of this democracy depends on how we use it, [...] democracy isn't automatic. It has to be nurtured[2], it has to be tended to[3], we have to work hard at it. [...] That's where real courage comes from. Not from turning on each other, but by turning toward one another. Not by sowing[4] hatred and division, but by spreading love and truth. Not by avoiding our responsibilities to create a better America and a better world, but by embracing those responsibilities through joy, perseverance, and discovering that in our beloved community, we do not walk alone."
>
> Barack Obama, eulogy for John Lewis[5], 30 July 2020; Transkript: Joshua Bote, https://eu.usatoday.com/story/news/politics/2020/07/30/barack-obama-eulogy-john-lewis-funeral-full-transcript/5544048002 [07.08.2020]

Although Obama never mentions President Trump's name, his remarks indirectly express scathing (*vernichtend*) criticism of Trump's policy.

Discuss in class whether (or not) you share Obama's view of democracy and how it has to be kept alive.

1 With the infection rate exploding and the economy in collapse, Donald Trump has failed spectacularly as a crisis manager. It would probably take a massive shock for him to get re-elected, but it appears he's trying to make that happen, too.

An American president setting off a war somewhere in the world to win an election he thinks is already lost – it's a script familiar to moviegoers. But an American president who threatens to wage war on American cities to turn an election campaign around? That's unheard of.

At least it was until now.

2 Amidst the clouds of tear gas, anonymous federal police in battle gear throw stun grenades[6] into a crowd, arresting protesters in the streets, locking them up without warrants[7]. The videos showing the deployment[8] of militarized troops in the United States look like scenes from the combat video game "Call of Duty." But they're real.

Donald Trump has deployed the federal troops from his Department of Homeland Security as a kind of presidential militia in Portland on the West Coast, where they have been using brute force[9] against Black Lives Matter supporters who have been protesting in the city for weeks. The heavily armed security force is usually reserved for things like counter-terrorism operations or going up against drug smugglers. They are in plain clothes and their vehicles have no license plates.

Every day, hundreds of mothers are peacefully standing up to the authorities. They call themselves the "wall of moms" and sing "please don't shoot us" and nursery rhymes[10]. But the security forces have no regard for[11]

Wall of Moms in Portland

[1] **the last stand** the final battle which is often hopeless – [2] **to nurture** to help a plan to develop and be successful – [3] **to tend to sb./sth.** (*phr. v.*) to deal with the problems or needs of a person or thing – [4] **to sow** *säen* – [5] **John Lewis** (1940–2020) African-American politician and civil rights activist – [6] **stun grenade** *Blendgranate* – [7] **warrant** *Haftbefehl* – [8] **deployment** the movement of soldiers or equipment to a place where they can be used when they are needed – [9] **brute force** great physical force or strength – [10] **nursery rhyme** *Kinderlied* – [11] **regard for sb./sth.** respect for sb./sth.

them. “Every night, moms have been teargassed, moms have been arrested, moms have been treated violently,” Joselyn Merrill, one of the protesting moms, says by phone. Merrill is an Air Force veteran with three children.

“A member of my congregation, who is also a city commissioner, was teargassed,” says Merrill. “The street medics[12] have also been targeted. These are people that are volunteering their time to make sure that everybody’s safety is of the foremost importance every night. It’s shocking that this is happening.”

Merrill says she took an oath on the Constitution as an Air Force veteran. “I never thought that this was going to happen on U.S. soil.”

The president, who is lagging far behind[13] challenger Joe Biden of the Democratic Party in virtually all polls[14], is doing something that none of his predecessors has done: He’s invading American cities. “We’ll do something,” Trump said. New York, Chicago, Philadelphia, Detroit and Baltimore, he said, are ruled by “liberal Democrats,” by the “radical left.” He argued that if Biden wins the presidency, the same would happen in the rest of the country. “The whole country would go to hell. And we’re not going to let it go to hell.”

Portland was the start. The president now wants to turn to cities where he believes there’s too much crime, which has in fact gone up in some places during the pandemic. But the fight against crime is normally the responsibility of the local police, with federal forces usually only stepping in if they are requested by local authorities. On Wednesday, Trump announced a “surge[15],” a military term from the Iraq war period that describes a massive increase in the number of troops with the goal of pacifying[16] the country. Hundreds of federal officers are now heading to cities like Chicago.

Critics warn that Trump, who is not exactly coming across[17] as sane[18] in the White House these days, is sowing the chaos[19] only so that he can then portray himself as a savior. Earlier this week, leftist *New York Times* columnist Michelle Goldberg wrote: “Trump’s occupation of American cities has begun.”

It feels like the last stand of a failed leader hoping for some major event to happen that would enable him to get re-elected in November – like fighting in the streets, or maybe even a miracle.

3 Historical Failure

Donald Trump’s presidential campaign is marked by a historical failure. The man who sold himself as a born manager literally fell apart when America faced its biggest crisis. COVID-19 has laid bare[20] Trump’s talents as president – which is to say, a complete lack thereof. It has also horrified many of his former voters.

He publicly suggested that injecting bleach could help protect against the virus and said that he told his people to test less in the country – since the problem for him wasn’t the many people who are sick, but rather the number of people being tested.

The number of COVID-19 deaths in the country is nearing the 150,000 mark. The COVID-19 pandemic has pushed around 30 million Americans into unemployment and robbed 5 million of their health insurance. With the rising number of infections preventing the economy from getting back on track, the recession is increasingly eating away at the American middle class.

The idea that the U.S. is a special nation is deeply anchored in the American soul. Under Trump, however, the word exceptionalism[21] has taken on a whole new meaning. No developed nation has managed the COVID-19 crisis as terribly as the U.S.: The country of 330 million is counting 66,000 new infections per day. In the European Union, which is home to 446 million people, the daily new infections number less than 5,000.

Federal law enforcement agents in Portland: "Trump’s occupation of American cities has begun."

[12] **street medic** (*AE*) a volunteer who helps at protests and demonstrations to provide medical care, for example first aid – [13] **to lag behind** *zurückbleiben hinter* – [14] **poll** *Umfrage* – [15] **surge** a sudden and great move forward – [16] **to pacify** to bring peace or end a war – [17] **to come across** (*phr. v.*) to behave in a way that makes people believe that you have a particular characteristic – [18] **sane** having a healthy mind – [19] **to sow chaos** *Chaos säen* – [20] **to lay bare sth.** to make sth. known – [21] **exceptionalism** the idea that a person, country or political system can be allowed to be different from, and perhaps better than, others

The U.S.'s top pandemic expert, Anthony Fauci, one of the last remaining voices of reason in the Trump administration, has described it as a "nightmare." This prompted[22] Trump's press team to start a campaign against the immunologist, who did nothing more than state things as they are, scientifically. That alone was enough to attract Trump's ire.

4 Holy War

The coronavirus pandemic could have been the opportunity for Trump to show that he was a crisis-capable president who transcended[23] party politics. In the end, nothing could have been further from the truth. Trump turned the fight against the virus into a holy war in which the mask was a symbol. For months, the president refused to wear one. The message he sent was clear: Only liberal weaklings who are susceptible[24] to the propaganda of the left-wing mainstream media wear masks. There are countless videos online in which furious Trump supporters defend their right to mask-free shopping. [...]

But after businesses and restaurants reopened, the numbers of infections went up again – partly because many refused to wear a mask. Now, Louisiana is the state in which the number of daily new infections is growing second-fastest in the country, after Florida. [...]

5 Devastating Poll Figures

Is a president with this kind of disastrous record even re-electable? If common sense and the rules of politics still mean anything, Trump should lose on Nov. 3. His poll numbers are almost at an all-time low. No president since Jimmy Carter[25] has had such devastating numbers. In the national polls, Trump is on average trailing[26] behind Biden by 9 percentage points. As things stand now, Biden would also win the crucial[27] swing states[28] of Pennsylvania, Wisconsin and Ohio.

It is mainly older voters and whites with a college degree who are turning on Trump. His core voters, whites without college educations, are still sticking with him, but based on the polls, he has even lost support there. If Trump is disappointing even his most loyal voters, then he has serious problems.

"Polling is inexact, you have to be careful how you interpret it. There are just so many moving parts," says Micah Cohen, one of the senior editors at FiveThirtyEight, a leading American poll-tracking website. "Trump is down by enough that it would take a historically huge polling error for him to win again like in 2016." [...]

6 "Scripted[29] Trump"

It was a new Donald Trump who appeared in the White House Press Room on Tuesday. "I have no problem with the masks," said the man who helped politicize masks more than anyone else in the U.S. But now he was playing a different tune: that "anything that potentially can help is a good thing." He also said he has a mask himself, which he wears in elevators.

Trump sounded calm, reasonable, almost boring. The wall behind him showed the infection curves – a graph that has become a kind of fever curve for his presidency – that he liked to keep quiet about during earlier press briefings.

Did the U.S. suddenly have a new, reformed president? A leader one could trust to lead the country through the terrible crisis?

This new Trump could be called the "scripted Trump," a man who listlessly[30] reads what others have written for him, a Trump who popped up especially often during the 2016 election campaign, when his advisers believed that it was best to hide the real Trump. [...]

7 An Apocalyptic Air

In recent days, he hasn't just been plagued by the polls – his appearances have also had an apocalyptic air to them. [...] There have also been devastating[31] books published by his former National Security Advisor John Bolton and his niece Mary Trump, both of whom portray the president as mentally incompetent.

And finally, Trump gave a devastating interview to journalist Chris Wallace of Fox News, usually his favorite channel. It marked a rare moment in which a journalist from the station questioned the president's statements and thwarted[32] his performance with precise questions. The president went off the rails[33], seeming tired and irritable[34].

[22] **to prompt** to make sth. happen – [23] **to transcend** to go further, rise above, or be more important or better than sth. – [24] **susceptible** [sə'septəbəl] easily influenced or harmed by sth. – [25] **Jimmy Carter** (*1924) American Democratic politician; 39th US President (1971 – 1975) – [26] **to be trailing** to be losing to your opponent in a competition, game or election – [27] **crucial** extremely important or necessary – [28] **swing state** a state where the number of Democratic and Republican voters is about the same, that has an important influence on the result of the election of the U.S. President – [29] **scripted** written down – [30] **listlessly** exhausted, without energy or enthusiasm – [31] **devastating** causing a lot of damage or destruction – [32] **to thwart** to stop sb. from doing sth. – [33] **to go off the rails** (*infml.*) to start behaving in a way that is not generally acceptable, especially dishonestly or illegally – [34] **irritable** *gereizt, auffahrend*

Trump made it clear that he might not accept defeat in the election, and Wallace confronted him about his false claim that Joe Biden wants to abolish the police. Trump also repeated that he had passed a cognitive test that he claimed Biden would be unlikely to pass. The Montreal Cognitive Assessment is designed to detect early forms of dementia in patients – and, contrary to what Trump may think, it is not an IQ test.

The journalist had to point out to Trump that the test was very simple, and merely required someone to, for example, recognize a drawing of an elephant. Nevertheless, the president boasted[35] in another interview this week that, as part of the test, he had actually managed to memorize and repeat the words "person," "woman," "man," "camera" and "TV." The video became a viral sensation. [...]

8 Bankrupt as a Businessman and Politician

Perhaps the greatest misconception[36] about Donald Trump before he got elected as president was that, even though he didn't have experience as a politician, he was a good manager – a successful businessman and a self-made billionaire who knew about deals.

But that was wrong even then. Trump has never been a very successful entrepreneur. He inherited a large part of his fortune, more than $400 million, from his father. *The New York Times* has reported that his companies posted losses of a billion dollars in the 1980s and 1990s alone. Germany's Deutsche Bank, of all institutions, stepped in from the 1990s onward with loans[37] to the tune of[38] billions, long before Trump became president. Many of his companies went bankrupt, including three casinos in Atlantic City and the Plaza Hotel on Fifth Avenue in New York.

The stories of contractors[39] and subcontractors[40] Trump never paid are notorious[41].

But it took the coronavirus to unmask Trump for what he really is and for him to be stripped of[42] his apparent Midas touch[43], making it impossible to overlook the fact that Trump is bankrupt not only as a businessman, but also as a politician and president. [...]

9 Republicans Won't Revolt

So far, no high-ranking Republican politicians have turned their backs on Trump. The only issue on which several senators have contradicted him is masks and how to contain the virus. He doesn't need to fear a revolt against him in the Republican Party. Even if some members of the House and Senate are worried they will be voted out of office along with the president this autumn, they don't dare to oppose him because he's still highly popular at the grassroots level[44].

But a small group of Republicans have turned their back on Trump and the party, and have been fighting fiercely[45]. The most prominent anti-Trump organization is the Lincoln Project, which is run by former Republican campaign strategists and floods the net with videos aimed at the president.

"Something's wrong with Donald Trump," one video informs. "He's shaky[46]. Weak. Trouble speaking. Trouble walking." The whole thing is interspersed[47] with footage[48] of the president holding a glass to his mouth with two hands or walking down a ramp at the West Point Military Academy[49] on shaky legs. "We're not

Donald and Melania Trump at Mount Rushmore[50], where the president described a nascent[51] "far-left fascism[52]."

[35] **to boast** *prahlen* – [36] **misconception** *Irrglaube* – [37] **loan** *Darlehen, Kredit* – [38] **to the tune of** to the stated amount – [39] **contractor** *Vertragsfirma* – [40] **subcontractor** *Subunternehmen* – [41] **notorious** *berüchtigt* – [42] **to strip sb. of sth.** (*phr. v.*) to take sth. important, such as a title, away from sb. as a punishment – [43] **the Midas touch** [ˈmaɪdəs] a person that is financially successful in everything they do – [44] **grassroots level** the ordinary people in a society or an organization, especially a political party – [45] **fiercely** in a frightening, violent or powerful way – [46] **shaky** *wackeling, unsicher* – [47] **to intersperse** *hier und da einfügen* – [48] **footage** *Filmmaterial* – [49] **West Point Military Academy** highly prestigious military service academy, established in 1801 – [50] **Mount Rushmore** a colossal sculpture carved into the granite of Mount Rushmore in the Black Hills, South Dakota; the sculpture features the portraits of the presidents George Washington, Thomas Jefferson, Theodore Roosevelt and Abraham Lincoln – [51] **nascent** [ˈneɪsənt] (*fml.*) *entstehend* – [52] **far-left fascism** *extrem linker Faschismus*

doctors, but we're not blind," the narrator says. "It's time we talk about this. Donald Trump is not well."

Normally, Trump is the one casting doubts[53] about the physical and mental health of his political opponents. His Democratic Party challenger Joe Biden has never stooped to[54] that level, but the Lincoln Project has no qualms[55] about doing so. [...]

The Lincoln Project's videos are having an effect, too. At a major event in Tulsa, Trump spent 14 minutes explaining why he was walking down the ramp so slowly at West Point. Nothing could have shown as clearly how concerned his is about accusations that he has anything but perfect health. [...]

10 "It's the Economy, Stupid!"

Even if only a small percentage of people change sides or stay away from the polling booths in contested states like Wisconsin or Arizona, it would be enough to impede Trump's re-election. The fact that Biden is the Democratic candidate makes it easier for moderate Republican voters to oppose Trump, especially now that the president has lost his most important campaign argument: a booming economy. Before the coronavirus struck[56], unemployment in the U.S. was at 3.5 percent, the lowest it had been since the 1960s. [...]

According to estimates by the Aspen Institute, a prominent American think tank, around 20 million renters in the U.S. could be facing eviction[57] between now and the end of September. Even though the U.S. government has imposed[58] a partial[59] moratorium[60] on evictions and foreclosures during the crisis, those restrictions end this week. Other important aid measures are also threatening to run out soon.

"It's the economy, stupid," is probably the most famous piece of American campaign wisdom, reflecting the belief that no candidate can prevail[61] against poor economic figures. The remark is allegedly[62] attributable[63] to James Carville, the political strategist who helped steer Bill Clinton's successful election campaign in 1992 against George H.W. Bush. The latter's failure to get re-elected actually had more to do with the global recession than with Clinton's strength.

Bush Sr. was the last U.S. president to fail to land a second term. Trump could be the next. Carville, still a sought-after[64] politician commentator, recently said in a television interview that he was certain Trump has "no chance" of re-election in November. [...]

11 Trump Will Have to Hope for a Miracle

So, Trump will have to hope for a miracle – or for his opponent to stumble. Probably the greatest weakness the Democrats have right now is their own presidential candidate. Biden is 77 years old and already has two unsuccessful bids to become the Democratic presidential nominee behind him. Each time, he managed to stumble over himself. The fact that he got so far this time has less to do with Biden's skills than with the fact that the man who is called "Uncle Joe" within his party is the person the most people could live with as the Democrats' candidate.

And that's still no guarantee that he can prevail against Trump, who has proven more than once that he knows how to put up a fight.

Trump's great skill has always been his ability to massively divide the country. That's also likely the calculation behind the police operations in American cities. Not a day has passed in recent weeks without Trump calling on his supporters to join the culture war against a purported[65] "leftist mob" which, together with Biden, wants to "wipe out our history" and "defame[66] our heroes."

In his now infamous[67] 4th of July speech at Mt. Rushmore, Trump even went so far as to claim "there is a new far-left fascism" on the rise in America and that he's the only one who can stop it. He said the leftists are not only determined to tear down statues of generals from the South who once defended slavery, but also those of historical presidents like George Washington and Thomas Jefferson because they had themselves been slave owners.

It sometimes seemed like Trump's primary interest was statues: He announced the creation of a statue park and said he wanted to use some of the statues at his campaign rallies. These days, however, one bust[68] seems to be more endangered that all the others: his own.

SPIEGEL.DE, 24. Juli 2020; https://www.spiegel.de/international/world/trump-s-handling-of-the-coronavirus-could-cost-him-the-presidency-a-341ffd75-5aba-46c9-983a-d063178512dd [25.07.2020]

[53] **to cast doubts** *Zweifel schüren* – [54] **to stoop to sth.** (*phr. v.*) to lower your moral standards by doing sth. that is unpleasant, dishonest, or unfair – [55] **qualm** *Skrupel* – [56] **to strike (struck, struck)** to hit or attack sb. – [57] **eviction** the act of forcing sb. to leave somewhere – [58] **to impose** to officially force a rule, tax, punishment, etc. to be obeyed or received – [59] **partial** not complete – [60] **moratorium** *Stillhalteabkommen* – [61] **to prevail** (*fml.*) to get control or influence – [62] **allegedly** *angeblich* – [63] **attributable** *zuschreibbar* – [64] **sought-after** *begehrt* – [65] **purported** *angeblich* – [66] **to defame** to damage the reputation of a person – [67] **infamous** famous for sth. considered bad – [68] **bust** a model of the head and shoulders of a person; *Büste*

COMPREHENSION

The magazine article at hand offers quite a comprehensive overview and analysis of Donald Trump, his past as a businessman, his presidency, and his chances of being re-elected in November 2020.

1. Read the introductory (first) part of the article and state which key problems and aspects concerning the U. S. and President Trump are depicted.

2. Divide the class into ten teams, preferably of two students each, with each team working with one paragraph from the article.
   Each team should make notes on a sheet of paper/a poster, which will then be attached to the board and will make up one part of a mind map depicting the most relevant aspects mentioned in the article.

   Step 1:
   Read your assigned paragraph first, and then clarify possible questions and/or unknown vocabulary.

   Step 2:
   @ If necessary, do further research on the topic of your paragraph and add further relevant information.

   Step 3:
   Think of an appropriate headline for your paragraph. You might even want to change the headlines given by the authors.

   Step 4:
   Attach your posters to the board, preferably in the pattern of a mind map, i. e. with topics and sub-topics. For example:

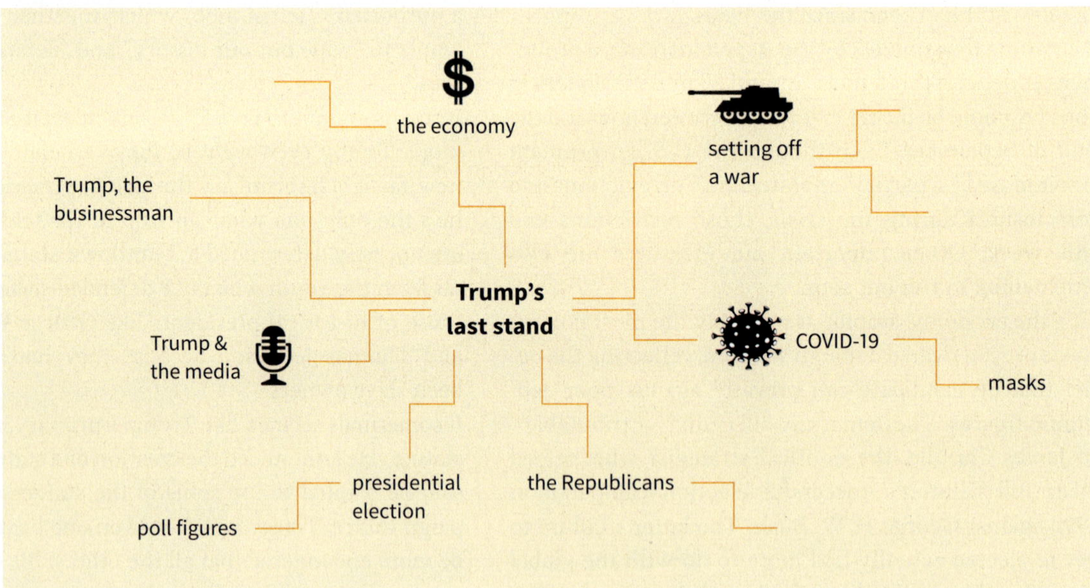

   Step 5:
   As a team, briefly present your findings to the class, highlighting the most relevant aspects.

3. Pick four paragraphs (topics) from the article that you consider the most important and summarize them in about 200 words.

   Tip: Do not forget to begin your summary with an introductory sentence that answers the w-questions (who – what – where – when – why) and use the simple present as the predominant tense.

ANALYSIS

4. Go through the article again and examine the arguments the authors have collected in favour of and against a second presidential term for Trump.
Juxtapose the most important arguments given and rank them according to how important the factors are for Trump's re-election.

5. Examine the style of the article and the authors' credibility.
Which rhetorical and/or stylistic devices were employed by the authors
a) to convey a certain message, but
b) to also appear credible and competent at the same time?

6. Choose one of the photographs (pp. 69, 70, 72) that you consider to be most telling and expressive with regard to the information given in the article and
a) describe it in detail,
b) explain its implicit symbolism and message.

ACTIVITIES

@ **7.** Do further research on Barack Obama's eulogy (*Trauerrede*) for John Lewis, one of the most important African-American civil rights activists and a companion of Martin Luther King.
You can either listen to Obama's eulogy or read the full transcript via these links:
- https://eu.usatoday.com/story/news/politics/2020/07/30/barack-obama-eulogy-john-lewis-funeral-full-transcript/5544048002/
- https://www.youtube.com/watch?v=QAnaFwehJW4 (41:00 mins)

Prepare a short presentation on what Obama
a) praises John Lewis, his life and work for,
b) criticizes about Trump and his politics,
c) wants to change concerning elections in the U. S.,
d) deems important for the future of the U. S.

Mariam Lau, Aminata Touré

Wildfremde[1] Leute fassen einem in die Haare

AWARENESS

@ Do research on Aminata Touré (*1992), her political work and career and prepare a short presentation for your class.

DIE ZEIT: Frau Touré, haben Sie in Deutschland rassistische Erfahrungen gemacht?
Aminata Touré: Ja, natürlich habe ich die gemacht. Ich berichte darüber nicht gern, weil das verletzende[2] und traumatisierende[3] Erfahrungen sind. Im Kieler Landtag habe ich mal gesagt, dass ich es hasse, darüber zu reden, weil die Leute einen dann immer so mitleidig[4] angucken. Und genau darum geht es mir überhaupt nicht. Es geht um kollektive Erfahrungen, die alle schwarzen Menschen kennen: als Abgeordnete[5] eine Wohnung nicht kriegen und vom Vermieter[6] zu hören bekommen, es wolle keine schwarzen Menschen haben. Wildfremde Leute fassen einem in die Haare. Man wird gefragt, wo man herkommt.

[1] completely strange – [2] hurtful – [3] traumatizing – [4] pitiful – [5] delegate – [6] landlord

ZEIT: Wenn jetzt weltweit Menschen mit denselben Losungen[7] und Plakaten protestieren: Ist Rassismus überall gleich?

Touré: Es gibt unterschiedliche Zustände, unterschiedliche Formen von Rassismus. Das Ausmaß an Polizeigewalt in den USA ist nicht vergleichbar mit dem in Deutschland, schlicht was die Zahl der Menschen betrifft, die da ums Leben kommen. Aber was man definitiv vergleichen kann, das ist die Struktur, die all dem zugrunde liegt – und das ist der Rassismus. Genau deshalb ist das auch eine weltweite Bewegung.

ZEIT: „Deutschlands Schwarze sind die Türken", war jetzt vereinzelt[8] zu lesen. Was halten Sie davon?

Touré: Gar nichts. Die Schwarzen sind die Schwarzen! [...]

ZEIT: Fühlen Sie sich wohl, wenn Plakate mit der Losung „All Cops Are Bastards" getragen werden?

Touré: Ich selbst würde ein solches Plakat nicht tragen. Ich bin Politikerin. Ich will innerhalb der Strukturen arbeiten. Ich bin mit der Polizei hier in Schleswig-Holstein in einem engen und regelmäßigen Austausch. Wir sprechen sehr offen über Rassismus. Ich werde da nichts beschönigen[9]. Im Umgang mit Konservativen und leider auch mit Liberalen merke ich oft, dass die jede Debatte totmachen[10] wollen, als dürfe man bloß kein kritisches Wort über die Polizei verlieren. Ich finde das völlig absurd, denn die Diskussionen, die ich mit der Polizei selbst habe, sind da sehr viel offener, selbstkritischer. Die wissen es absolut zu schätzen, wenn man da Klartext[11] redet.

ZEIT: Haben Sie dafür Beispiele?

Touré: Ich habe im Februar mit Ministerpräsident Daniel Günther eine Patenschaft übernommen[12] für die Polizeischule Eutin mit „Schule ohne Rassismus – Schule mit Courage". Es ist die erste Polizeischule[13], die bei diesem Projekt mitmacht. Wir haben mit den Schülern und auch mit der Leitung über rassistische und sexistische Vorfälle geredet: über Chats, die es gab, oder über einen schwarzen Polizeischüler[14], der aufgegeben hat. [...] Für alle Institutionen, von Polizei über Justiz bis zur Verwaltung – also überall dort, wo der Staat selbst in der Verantwortung steht – muss es Fort- und Weiterbildungen[15] zu diesem Thema geben. In Schleswig-Holstein haben wir für den Justizbereich[16] eine Zusammenarbeit mit dem Deutschen Institut für Menschenrechte, wo das Justizpersonal[17] für Rassismus sensibilisiert wird. In der Zivilgesellschaft[18] wünsche ich mir, dass Menschen einschreiten, wenn sie Rassismus mitbekommen. Dass sie zuhören und sich klarmachen, dass all das nicht nur Minderheiten etwas angeht, sondern die Grundfesten[19] der Demokratie betrifft. Bildung zum Thema Kolonialismus – das ist eine Länderaufgabe[20], die wir hier kommende Woche in Angriff nehmen. [...]

ZEIT: In Antirassismus-Trainings lernen Teilnehmer, sich als Angehörige von Rassen zu verstehen: als Weiße, als People of Colour. Ist das wirklich ein Fortschritt – oder nicht vielmehr der Weg in die Stammesgesellschaft[21]?

Touré: Auch wenn das kleinlich[22] klingt: Ich würde nie von „Rassen" sprechen, weil damit das Problem überhaupt erst anfängt. Ich habe selbst mehrere solcher Workshops gegeben and Schulen und Unis. Es geht erst einmal darum, das alles historisch einzuordnen[23], so wie wir das beim Antisemitismus[24] auch tun. Zu wissen: Woher kommt der ganze Scheiß eigentlich, wie kommt es, dass wir das alles einfach so unreflektiert[25] im Kopf haben? In den Schulen muss zum Beispiel über Kolonialismus oder Sklavenhandel geredet werden. Es geht nicht darum, die Menschen in unterschiedliche Kategorien einzuteilen. Aber ich kann die vielen Male gar nicht mehr zählen, in denen Gesprächspartner völlig überrascht davon waren, wenn ich sie als weiß bezeichnet habe. Das ist für mich keine Beleidigung[26], es ist ein Fakt. Genauso wie ich das seit 27 Jahren kenne, dass Menschen feststellen, dass ich schwarz bin, und mich fragen, woher ich komme. Wir alle haben eine bestimmte Position, bestimmt Privilegien, bestimmte Erfahrungen.

ZEIT: Sie halten also das Ziel einer „farbenblinden[27]" Gesellschaft, wie der klassische Liberalismus sie fordert, für nicht angemessen[28]?

Touré: Es gibt verschiedene Etappen. Am Ende muss stehen, dass diese Kategorien keine Rolle mehr spielen. Aber auf dem Weg dorthin müssen wir uns über unsere Positionierung[29] ich der Gesellschaft klar werden. Viele würden für sich sagen: Hautfarbe spielt keine Rolle – Ich bin Weltbürgerin[30]. Ich war auch schon mal in Ghana, ich war in Kinshasa. Das ist löblich[31]. Aber die Situation einer schwarzen Person, die morgens auf die Straße tritt, ist eine völlig andere. Wer das nicht sieht, weil er sich anders positioniert, ignoriert Lebensrealitäten.

Mariam Lau im Interview mit Aminata Touré: „Wildfremde Leute fassen einem in die Haare", DIE ZEIT 25/2020 (Auszug)

[7] slogan – [8] occasionally – [9] to gloss over – [10] to kill – [11] to speak plainly to one another – [12] to sponsor sb./sth. – [13] police academy – [14] police trainee – [15] training and development – [16] judiciary – [17] judicial employees/personnel – [18] civil society – [19] foundations – [20] responsibility of the German federal states – [21] tribal society – [22] pedantic – [23] to put in their correct order– [24] antisemitism – [25] withour thinking – [26] insult – [27] colour blind – [28] appropriate – [29] positioning – [30] cosmopolitan – [31] praiseworthy

COMPREHENSION

Scenario:
Your American exchange student Simon has heard about Black Lives Matter demonstrations in many German cities in support of and solidarity with the American civil rights movement. He found this interview online but his knowledge of German is not good enough to fully understand it. Guessing from the photograph, what he read about Aminata Touré on the internet and some German words he knows, he asks whether there is racism and harassment of black people in Germany as well.

1. In a first reading of the article, find information about
- Touré's experiences with racism in Germany
- Touré's view of racism worldwide
- Touré's cooperation with the police
- her political work in Schleswig-Holstein
- why teaching students about colonialism at school is important
- the importance of skin colour.

2. Next, make notes on these aspects in English.

ANALYSIS

3. Team up with a partner and
a) describe the photos, which were taken in German cities shortly after the killing of George Floyd,
b) explain the messages the protesters wanted to convey.

Demonstration in the city of Mannheim; the participants were asked to dress in black; most of the participants also wear masks because of the coronavirus regulations.

Demonstration in the city of Frankfurt; protesters are carrying placards.

Tips on vocab

to raise one's fist ■ to kneel down ■ to take a knee ■ to show respect and solidarity ■ to kneel side by side ■ to be dressed in black

Tips on vocab

downtown Frankfurt ■ skyline of historic houses ■ to carry/hold up placards ■ to identify oneself with sth./sb.

ACTIVITIES

4. Now, write an email to your friend Simon and tell him about racism in Germany and how a black German politician is trying to bring about change by setting an example.

Ta-Nehisi Coates

Between the World and Me

AWARENESS

In his 2015 autobiographical book, written as a letter to his teenage son, African American writer Ta-Nehisi Coates reflects on his feelings, the realities associated with being black in the U. S. and the seemingly never-ending white supremacy. The title of Ta-Nehisi's book derives from a poem by Richard Wright, published in 1935, which deals with a black man discovering the site of a lynching.

Step 1: Access the website https://www.poemhunter.com/poem/between-the-world-and-me/ and find out what exactly the speaker of the poem describes.

Step 2: Speculate about why Coates might have chosen this poem as the inspiration to write a book about contemporary America for his then 15-year-old son.

1 I write you in your fifteenth year. I am writing you because this was the year I saw Eric Garner choked[1] to death for selling cigarettes; because you know now that Renisha McBride was shot for seeking help, that John Crawford was shot down for browsing in a department store. And you have seen men in uniform drive by and murder Tamir Rice, a twelve-year-old child whom they were oath-bound to protect. And you have seen men in the same uniforms pummel[2] Marlene Pinnock, someone's grandmother, on the side of a road. And you know now, if you did not before, that the police departments of your country have been endowed[3] with the authority to destroy your body. It does not matter if the destruction is the result of an unfortunate overreaction. It does not matter if it originates in a misunderstanding. It does not matter if the destruction springs from a foolish policy. Sell cigarettes without the proper authority and your body can be destroyed. Resent[4] people trying to entrap[5] your body and it can be destroyed. Turn into a dark stairwell and your body can be destroyed. The destroyers will rarely be held accountable[6]. Mostly they will receive pensions. And destruction is merely the superlative form of a dominion[7] whose prerogatives[8] include friskings[9], detainings[10], beatings, and humiliations[11]. All of this is common to black people. And all of this is old for black people. No one is held responsible. [...] (p. 8)

2 I came out of the studio and walked for a while. It was a calm December day. Families, believing themselves white, were out on the streets. Infants, raised to be white, were bundled in strollers[12]. And I was sad for these people, much as I was sad for [...] all the people out there watching and reveling[13] in a specious[14] hope. I realized then why I was sad. When the journalist asked me about my body, it was like she was asking me to awaken her from the most gorgeous[15] dream. I have seen that dream all my life. It is perfect houses with nice lawns. It is Memorial Day[16] cookouts[17], block associations, and driveways. The Dream is treehouses and the Cub Scouts[18]. The Dream smells like peppermint but tastes like strawberry shortcake. And for so long I have wanted to escape into the Dream, to fold my country over my head like a blanket. But this has never been an option because the Dream rests on[19] our backs, the bedding[20] made from our bodies. And knowing this, knowing that the Dream persists[21] by warring with[22] the known world, I was sad [...] for all those families, I

[1] **to choke sb.** *jdn. ersticken* – [2] **to pummel** to hit sb./sth. repeatedly, esp. with your fists – [3] **to be endowed with** (*idm.*) to be given/provided with – [4] **to resent** to dislike or be angry at sth. or sb. because you have been hurt or not treated fairly – [5] **to entrap** to catch as if in a trap – [6] **accountable** responsible – [7] **dominion** the power or right to rule – [8] **prerogative** special right; *Vorrecht* – [9] **frisking** searching sb. for hidden weapons or goods by passing the hands over the body – [10] **detaining** preventing sb. from leaving for a certain time – [11] **humiliation** causing sb. to feel ashamed; not showing respect - [12] **stroller** *Kinderwagen* – [13] **to revel** to dance, drink, sing, etc. at a party or in public, especially in a noisy way – [14] **specious** (*fml.*) *trügerisch* – [15] **gorgeous** very beautiful and pleasant – [16] **Memorial Day** a US holiday on the last Monday in May when people remember men and women who have died, especially those who have died fighting for their country in wars – [17] **cookout** (*infml.*) a party at which food is cooked outdoors – [18] **Cub Scout** an organization modeled after the Boy Scouts (*Pfadfinder*) but for younger boys 7 to 10 years old – [19] **to rest on** to lean on/be supported by sb./sth. – [20] **bedding** *Unterlage, Lager* – [21] **to persist** to continue to exist – [22] **warring** disagreeing and arguing strongly with each other

was sad for my country, but above all, in that moment, I was sad for you. [...] (pp. 10/11)

3 Every February my classmates and I were herded into assemblies for a ritual review of the Civil Rights Movement. Our teachers urged us toward the example of freedom marchers, Freedom Riders[23], and Freedom Summers[24], and it seemed that the month could not pass without a series of films dedicated to the glories of being beaten on camera. The black people in these films seemed to love the worst things in life – love the dogs that rent their children apart[25], the tear gas that clawed[26] at their lungs, the firehoses[27] that tore off their clothes and tumbled them into the streets. They seemed to love the men who raped them, the women who cursed them, love the children who spat on them, the terrorists that bombed them. *Why are they showing this to us?* Why were only our heroes nonviolent? I speak not of the morality of nonviolence, but of the sense that blacks are in especial need of this morality. Back then all I could do was measure these freedom-lovers by what I knew. Which is to say, I measured them against children pulling out[28] in the 7-Eleven parking lot[29], against parents wielding[30] extension cords[31], and "Yeah, nigger, what's up now?" I judged them against the country I knew, which had acquired the land through murder and tamed it under slavery, against the country whose armies fanned out[32] across the world to extend their dominion. The world, the real one, was civilization secured and ruled by savage means. How could the schools valorize[33] men and women whose values society actively scorned[34]? How could they send us out into the streets of Baltimore, knowing all that they were, and then speak of nonviolence? [...] (pp. 31/32)

from *Between the World and Me* by Ta-Nehisi Coates. Spiegel & Grau International Edition, New York 2017, pp. 8, 10/11, 31/32

COMPREHENSION

1. Read the three excerpts from different parts of the book and get a first impression of Coates's feelings and concerns.

2. In order to get a deeper understanding of the author's motivation for writing this book to his son, do research on the people referred to in the **first part** of the excerpt, and find out who they are and what happened to them:
   - Eric Garner
   - Renisha McBride
   - John Crawford
   - Tamir Rice
   - Marlene Pinnock

3. What conclusions does the writer draw from these people's stories?

4. Present the author's observations of white Americans and the "Dream" as depicted in the **second part** of the excerpt.

5. Outline the author's reflections on the Civil Rights Movement in comparison to his world as a teenager growing up in Baltimore.

Civil Rights Movement ⟷	growing up in Baltimore
• Freedom marchers	• ...
• Freedom ...	• ...
• love the men who ...	• Nigger, what's up ...
• ...	• ...

[23] **Freedom Rider** a person who challenged segregation laws in the southern US states during the 1960s – [24] **Freedom Summer** nonviolent effort by civil rights activists to integrate Mississippi's segregated political system during 1964 – [25] **to rent apart** here: tear apart – [26] **to claw at sth.** *die Klauen nach etw. ausstrecken* – [27] **firehose** *Feuerwehrschlauch* – [28] **to pull out** (*phr. v.*) to leave a road and move onto a different road; *abfahren* – [29] **7-Eleven parking lot** car park of the 7-Eleven chain of convenience stores, which can be a hot spot of gang fights, drug dealing and confrontation with the police – [30] **to wield** to hold a weapon or tool and look as if you are going to use it – [31] **extension cord** *Verlängerungskabel* – [32] **to fan out** (*phr. v.*) to move in different directions from a single point – [33] **to valorize** *jdn./etw. aufwerten* – [34] **to scorn** *verachten*

ANALYSIS

6. The overall tone of these excerpts is melancholic and expresses a feeling of hopelessness and helplessness. Find examples of how the author uses stylistic devices and specific language to emphasize his emotions and view.

ACTIVITIES

7. Comment on and evaluate the excerpts from Ta-Nehisi Coates's book. Is he right in preparing his teenage son for a seemingly dangerous and prejudiced U. S./world or should he be more positive, comforting and encouraging? What conclusions do you assume will his son draw from his father's book?

Barrett Holmes Pitner

US Must Confront Its Original Sin to Move Forward

AWARENESS

a) What do you associate with the term 'original sin'?
b) Which events in history could be referred to when taking about
   - America's,
   - Germany's,
   - Britain's 'original sin'?

Discuss your ideas in class.

Following the death of George Floyd while under arrest, protests have consumed[1] America and onlookers have wondered how one of the most powerful countries in the world could descend[2] into such chaos.

Despite being defined by race, American society does not spend much time analysing the history of our racial divisions, and America prefers to believe in the inevitable[3] progression[4] towards racial equality.

The election of Barack Obama in 2008 fed into this narrative[5] of progress, but Donald Trump's presidential victory in 2016 was seen as a step backwards, coming after a campaign with a slogan that championed America's divisive[6] past as a form of progress.

Floyd's death now appears to be the tipping point for an exhausted, racially divided nation still in the throes[7] of the coronavirus pandemic and the economic cost that followed.

Protesters attacked by police dogs during demonstrations against segregation in Alabama in 1963

Floyd's cries of "I can't breathe" echoed the cries of Eric Garner, who was choked by police on a New York City sidewalk in 2014.

Floyd's words reminded Americans of the oppressive past we work to forget regardless of whether it is six years ago, 60 years ago, the 1860s, or 1619 when some of the first slaves arrived in America.

To a large extent, America's neglect[8] of the past and belief in progress have left many Americans unaware of the severity[9] and scope[10] of our racial tensions, and as a result many Americans lack the words to articulate our current turmoil. Recently, I have used the word ethnocide meaning "the destruction of culture while keeping the people" to de-

[1] **to consume** *verzehren* – [2] **to descend into sth.** (*phr. v.*) to become worse – [3] **inevitable** *unausweichlich* – [4] **progression** *Fortschreiten* – [5] **narrative** the story or description of historical events – [6] **divisive** causing disunity – [7] **in the throes** (*lit.*) struggling with – [8] **neglect** *Vernachlässigung* – [9] **severity** seriousness – [10] **scope** range; *Tragweite*

scribe America's past and present racial tensions, and this language also helps articulate the uniqueness of America's race problem.

In 1941, Raphael Lemkin, a Polish Jew and distinguished lawyer, immigrated to the United States as he fled the Nazis. While in America he implored the American government to stop the Nazis from killing his people, and as his words fell on deaf ears[11], he realized he needed to create a new word to describe the unique horror befalling his people. In 1944, Lemkin coined the words genocide and ethnocide.

Lemkin intended for the words to be interchangeable but over time they diverged[12]. Genocide became the destruction of a people and their culture, and this word radically changed the world for the better. Ethnocide became the destruction of culture while keeping the people, and has been ignored for decades. [...]

From the beginning of the transatlantic slave trade, European colonizers destroyed the culture of African people, but kept their bodies in order to create the chattel[13] slavery system that became the economic and social foundation of the United States. Colonizers prevented Africans from speaking their languages and practising their religions. Tribal[14] and familial bonds were broken, and African people could no longer identify as Igbo, Yoruba, and Malian. Instead de-cultured names such as nigger, negro, coloured, and black were stamped upon[15] African people.

Additionally, Europeans identified themselves as white, and in the United States the one-drop rule[16] was created to sustain[17] that division. One drop of black or African blood meant that a person could not be white. In America, whiteness became a zero-sum identity that was maintained by systemic racial division. Interracial marriage was still illegal in much of America until the Loving vs Virginia[18] decision in 1967.

From colonization to the formation of the United States, America has created countless laws and policies to sustain the racial division between blacks and whites forged[19] by ethnocide. These American norms, extending to housing, education, employment, healthcare, law

People demonstrating against the unfair treatment of black people

enforcement and environmental protections including clean drinking water, have disproportionately harmed African Americans and other communities of colour in order to sustain racial division and white dominance.

George Floyd's murder represents a continuation of the systemic criminalization and oppression of black life in America that has always been the American norm dating back to Jim Crow[20], segregation (which means apartheid), and slavery. [...]

Despite the American South losing the Civil War in 1865, American President Andrew Johnson[21] pardoned Confederate[22] soldiers, and soon thereafter Confederate politicians won elected office in the newly-reunited America. The influence of former slave owners and Confederates contributed to erasing[23] the rights that African Americans won in the 1860s including citizenship and the right to vote.

The political campaign to remove African American rights was called the Redeemers movement[24], and it was led by former slave-owners and Confederates, who wanted to redeem[25] the South by returning it to the norms of chattel slavery. [...]

The Redeemers were also assisted by American terrorist groups such as the Ku Klux Klan[26] (KKK) that were made up of former Confederate soldiers. The KKK, and

[11] **deaf** unable to hear; **to fall on deaf ears** to be ignored or paid no attention to – [12] **to diverge** to separate, become different – [13] **chattel** (*fml., old*) article of movable property – [14] **tribal** *Stammes-* – [15] **to stamp sth. upon sb.** (*phr. v.*) *jdm. etw. aufstempeln* – [16] **one-drop rule** a social and legal principle of racial classification in the early 20th century which asserted that any person with even one ancestor of black ancestry was considered black – [17] **to sustain** to keep alive – [18] **Loving vs. Virginia** (1967) U. S. Supreme Court decision against banning interracial marriage – [19] **to forge** to make or produce sth. – [20] **Jim Crow** local and state laws that enforced racial segregation in the U. S. South – [21] **President Andrew Johnson** (1808 – 1875) 17th president of the U. S. – [22] **Confederate** belonging to a a group of seven slave-holding states fighting against the 'Union' in the American Civil War – [23] **to erase** to remove sth. – [24] **Redeemers movement** a political coalition in the Southern U. S. which enforced white supremacy – [25] **to redeem** to get back – [26] **Ku Klux Klan** an American white supremacist, right-wing extremist and terrorist hate group

many other white supremacist groups, terrorized and lynched black Americans, and they also prevented them from voting to help ensure that Redeemer candidates won elected office. The terrorists became the government. [...]

According to the Equal Justice Initiative's 2017 report Lynching in America, over 4,400 lynchings of African Americans occurred from 1877 – 1950. That is more than a lynching a week for 74 years.

During Jim Crow, America could not legally deny black people their humanity, but they could deny them the services that are afforded[27] to human beings. Black people were denied education, housing, employment, and were expected to "know their place" as a perpetually[28] subjugated[29] people. Large prisons were erected on former plantations; black people were arrested for minor crimes and given long prison sentences doing manual labour on the same land their ancestors were forced to work as enslaved people.

As a result of Jim Crow, millions of African Americans fled the neo-slavery and terror of the South during the Great Migration[30], and racial tensions spread as other American cities did not welcome these domestic refugees. This is the same journey as the Underground Railroad, where prior to the Civil War enslaved African Americans escaped the South and sought refuge in Canada and the Northern parts of America.

The civil rights movement of the 1960s effectively ended Jim Crow, and African Americans began reclaiming the rights, specifically voting rights and freedom of movement, they had previously won in the 1860s, but it is a long road to dismantle[31] systemic and legalized racism and segregation. [...]

Obama's election in 2008 was a monumental event in American society, but it did not magically erase the systemic racism woven into America's social fabric[32] and the 2012 killing of Trayvon Martin[33], 17, helped launch the Black Lives Matter movement to national attention. [...]

The unjust killing of black people by the police and racist vigilantes[34] remained the norm during Obama's presidency, but now the black community could record and document these crimes on video, and had a president who would defend them. Obama famously said: "If I had a son, he'd look like Trayvon."

The emergence of the Black Lives Matter movement and other protests under Obama occurred because black Americans were confident[35] that the White House would listen to their cries of "I can't breathe" and make American society finally equitable[36] and just. Under Trump those cries have fallen on deaf ears and tensions have escalated. [...]

America has much work to do to fix our racial tensions because our divisions and inequality are forged in our ethnocidal roots. We need to reform the policing of a nation nearly the size of a continent with over 300 million people, but we also need to make our education, healthcare, and housing systems, and every facet[37] of our democracy more equitable. [...]

Also, America has rarely criminalized white supremacist hate and terror and instead has spent centuries normalizing white terrorist groups, celebrating them as heroes, and letting them decide if their actions are evil or not. This is why the Confederacy is still celebrated today. Europe did not allow fascists and Nazis to determine if their actions were good or not, but America has always given this luxury to racist slave-owners and their generational apologists[38] and offspring[39]. This must change.

Rwanda, Germany, and South Africa have reckoned[40] with their troubled past to make a better future, but America has long preferred to ignore the past, and proclaim the inevitability[41] of progress.

America today must define and confront the Original Sin of slavery, ethnocide, and the cultural destruction it has inflicted[42] upon all Americans, past and present. Otherwise we will fail to make a better future, and will continue our regression[43].

Barrett Holmes Pitner is a writer, journalist and filmmaker focusing on race, culture and politics.

https://www.bbc.com/news/world-us-canada-52912238 [10.06.2020]

[27] **to afford** to be able to buy or do sth. because you have enough time or money – [28] **perpetually** always or very often – [29] **to subjugate sb.** *unterwerfen, unterjochen* – [30] **Great Migration** (1916 – 1970) movement of aournd six million African Americans from the Southern rural U. S. to the urban, industrialized Northeast and Midwest – [31] **to dismantle** to get rid of a system or organization – [32] **fabric** the structure or parts of sth. – [33] **Trayvon Martin** 17-year-old African American who was shot by a white community watch in 2012 – [34] **vigilantes** *Bürgerwehr* – [35] **confident** *zuversichtlich* – [36] **equitable** treating everyone fairly and in the same way – [37] **facet** aspect – [38] **apologist** a person who supports a particular belief or political system, esp. an unpopular one, and speaks or writes in defence of it – [39] **offspring** a person's children – [40] **to reckon with** to deal with – [41] **inevitability** *Unausweichlichkeit* – [42] **to inflict upon** to force sb. to experience sth. very unpleasant – [43] **regression** (*fml.*) a return to a previous and less advanced or worse state, condition, or way of behaving

COMPREHENSION

1. The names and terms in the box below are taken from the BBC article on pp. 80 ff.

Black Lives Matter ● Trayvon Martin ● Obama Presidency ● Civil War ● Trump Presidency ● colonization ● Eric Garner ● first slaves ● Raphael Lemkin ● transatlantic slave trade ● slavery ● Jim Crow ● Loving vs. Virginia ● segregation ● Redeemers ● KKK ● lynchings ● Great Migration ● Underground Railroad ● Civil Rights Movement

Step 1: Together with a partner, scan the article and collect information given about the names and events in U. S. history.

Step 2: Draw a timeline and arrange the data and information given in chronological order.

Tip: Do further research on the internet to clarify or specify data or information given in the article. If you want, you can also add historical photographs/graphics or icons to your timeline.

Step 3: Present your timelines in class and inform each other about your findings.

2. Following his outline of (African) American history, the author sets up a list of needs and imperatives for the future. Specify this list of 'work to do' (ll. 163 ff.).

Tips on vocab

a gravesite ■ tombstone with an inscription (name and olive twig) ■ a clenched fist raising out of the ground/ grave ■ a lorry dumping soil on the grave ■ Trump looking like a gardener with a rake in his hand ■ to cover sth. up ■ to let the dust settle on sth. (*Gras über etw. wachsen lassen*)

ANALYSIS

3. In his concluding paragraph, (ll. 180 – 188), the author contrasts the way Europe, Rwanda, Germany and South Africa have come to terms with their past (*Vergangenheitsbewältigung*) with America's refusal to do so. Explain what, according to the author, is going wrong in the U. S. and why the above-mentioned countries could serve as role models.

M **4.** Describe the cartoon by German cartoonist Nik Ebert and explain how its message matches the observations and assessments made in the BBC article.

GRAS DRÜBER... 10.06.2020

ACTIVITIES

5. As a young student who has dealt with Germany's past and its 'original sin' in history lessons, and who lives in a more multicultural German society today, write a letter to the editor in response to the article in which you state your view on the subject.

Acknowledgements

Images

|Alamy Stock Photo, Abingdon/Oxfordshire: Dagnall, Ian 17; Garcia, Mariano 30; GL Archive 42; Lebrecht Music & Arts 21; North Wind Picture Archives 22; Photo 12 34; PictureLux/The Hollywood Archive 42; Purestock 23; White House Photo 38. |Alamy Stock Photo (RMB), Abingdon/Oxfordshire: age fotostock 18. |Bell, Steve, Brighton: 64. |Cagle Cartoons, Santa Barbara, CA: Bagley, Pat 45; Beeler, Nate 56; Fitzsimmons, David 6; Granlund, Dave 28, 32, 45; McKee, Rick 56; Sack, Steve 4; Whamond, Dave 51; Wilkinson, Signe 32. |Catprint Media GmbH, Langenhagen: Landschulz, Dorthe 66. |Courtesy of Pest Control Office - Banksy, London: 2020 15. |Der Spiegel, Hamburg: SPIEGEL 24/2020 8, 9; SPIEGEL 25/2020 33. |Domke, Franz-Josef, Hannover: 29, 29, 29. |Ebert, Nik, Mönchengladbach: Rheinische Post 83. |Getty Images, München: AFP/Uzcategui, Eva Marie 59; Afro American Newspapers/Gado 80; Bettmann Archive 81; McNamee, Win 65. |Globe Cartoon, Geneva: © Chappatte, Der Spiegel, www.chappatte.com 11, 51. |Picture-Alliance GmbH, Frankfurt/M.: AP Photo/Ceneta, Manuel Balce 59; AP Photo/Sanchez, Marcio Jose 69; AP Photo/Semansky, Patrick 62; AP Photo/Wong Maye-E 4; dieKLEINERT.de/Schwarwel 26; dpa/Anspach, Uwe 77; dpa/EPA/Mabanglo, John G 60; dpa/Roessler, Boris 77; Geisler-Fotopress/gbrci 75; REUTERS/Ochs, Caitlin 70; ZUMA Press/White House/Hanks, Andrea 72. |stock.adobe.com, Dublin: Abolins, Janis 32; designua 74; elchinjafarli 74; fersus art 74; Hoeda80 74; LCosmo 83; Premium Icons 32; Uqierese 32; WC 24 83. |Stuttmann, Klaus, Berlin: 66. |twitter.com: 51, 51, 54.